Fire in the Bowl
Favorite Chili Recipes and More

Compiled by Carol Blakely

Associate editors: Melinda Bradnan, Miriam Canter, Dorothy C
Schnoebelen, Deb Schense, Dwayne and Joan Liffring-Zug
Cover graphics: M. A. Cook Design;   Interior Drawings: Diane
Photography: Joan Liffring-Zug Bourret;   Woodcut: Esthe

Penfield Books

The Delicious World of Penfield Books

Front cover: The plate, purchased from a beach vendor, shows chiles from western Mexico.

Back cover: The red chile wreath, purchased from *Made in New Mexico*, is made only from the bright red fresh piquin peppers grown for centuries in the Mesilla Valley region of southern New Mexico.

Penfield Books, 215 Brown Street, Iowa City, IA 52245-5801
www.penfieldbooks.com • 1-800-728-9998 • penfield@penfieldbooks.com
ISBN: 978-1932043648   © 2010 Penfield Books   Printed in the U. S. A.

About the Compiler

Carol Blakely, of Dallas, Texas, started helping her mother and grandmother in the kitchen around the age of seven. Her first cooking success was a fresh orange cake that she baked from scratch when she was nine. By the time she was eleven, she was preparing a complete Sunday dinner for her large family. Carol states that she always wants to know the "story" behind a certain food or recipe, and her files are full of cooking notes, the history of foods and food customs.

She continued her cooking hobby through college, raising a family and working for many years as a software consultant. In the late 1990s, she turned to the Internet to share her love of food and cooking with her web site, The Jalapeño Café. The Jalapeño Café is devoted to Southwestern and Mexican cooking with music, poems, and images about food and lifestyles in the Southwest. There is a top ten list of Mexican cookbooks, plus interesting facts relating to Southwest food customs. One section is devoted to chili recipes.

Carol continues to spend her spare time in the kitchen trying out new recipes and cooking for friends and family.

Contents

Dried red chile peppers tied into ristras *with a green bell pepper shown in the center*

Introduction

Although many people think chili is a Mexican dish, it is a true Texas dish, yet its origins are shrouded in mystery. Some say it was first made by chuckwagon cooks who picked wild peppers along the cattle trails to add to their beef stews. Others say it originated with the Chili Queens in their open-air food stands in the plazas of San Antonio. Still others say it originated in the Texas jails where the sheriff's wife used chiles to disguise the taste of not so fresh and inferior meats served to the prisoners. My own feeling is that it's a combination of all these factors. In 1977, the Texas legislature designated chili as the official food of Texas, and you can be sure that at any given time, somewhere in Texas, someone is eating a bowl of chili. Chili is a hearty dish, real-man food, tailgate-party food, blue norther food, snowy day food. It is not a dish to serve on a lace tablecloth by candlelight, but on the bare planks of a picnic table or on the back of a pick-up truck.

Chile Heat Scale

Heat Rating:	Chile Varieties:
10 Hottest	Bahamian, Habañero
9	Japanese Santaka, Chiltecpin, Thai
8	Cayenne, Tabasco
7	de Arbol, (Pequin/Piquin)
6	Yellow Wax, Serrano
5	Jalapeño, Mirasol
4	Sandia, Cascabel, Chipotle, Poblano
3	Ancho, Pasilla
2	Rio Grande, Big Jim, Anaheim, NM-6
1	R-Naky, El Paso, Cherry, New Mexico
0 No Heat	Bells, Pimiento, Sweet Banana

Chiles Used in This Cookbook

Listed below are the chile peppers used in the recipes in this cookbook. Most are available at local supermarkets. If they are not available in your area, they can be ordered from many sources on the Internet.

Fresh Chiles

Serrano - A thin green chile about two inches long, is a little hotter than a jalapeño, and can be used when jalapeños are called for. Looks similar to a jalapeño pepper.

Anaheim - Also called the California chile is a large pepper about seven inches long. It is one of the mildest chiles. Canned green chiles are usually Anaheim peppers.

(continued)

Fresh Chiles *(continued)*

Poblano - A deep green large chile about five inches long and wider than most chiles. This is a favorite for New Mexico green-chile stews.

New Mexico Green Chiles - This chile is about five or six inches long and is hotter than the Anaheim, but not as hot as the jalapeño. The best New Mexico green chiles are grown in the Hatch Valley. New Mexico green chiles are sold frozen in some stores.

Habañero - This reddish-orange pepper looks like a shriveled bell pepper, but is extremely hot. It is usually used raw and is used in salsas.

Jalapeño - This is the most popular green chile pepper in America. It is used fresh or often pickled and added to many cooked dishes. The pepper is usually two to three inches long and is medium hot.

To Roast Green Chiles

The skin of fresh green chiles should be removed before using, especially from Anaheim and New Mexico green peppers. Jalapeños and serranos do not usually need to have their skin removed if chopped fine. Before roasting, cut a slit in each chile to keep it from bursting.

Broiler: Place chiles on broiler pan and place under broiler that has been pre-heated for 10 minutes. Watch closely, turning frequently so the chiles are charred and blistered on all sides.

Gas Burner: If you have a gas stove, you can char chiles over the gas flame, using tongs to hold and rotate the chile until its skin blisters and is charred all over.

(continued)

To Roast Green Chiles *(continued)*

Once the chiles are charred, place them in a paper or plastic bag for 20 to 30 minutes so the steam will continue to loosen the skins. Once the skin is loosened, it should peel away from the chile easily. Rinse the chile and break the stem away. Slice open and scrape away the seeds and ribs.

Dried Chiles

Chile de Arbol - Thin red chiles, these are the ripe, dried version of the serrano and are very hot. They are commonly used in pickles and relishes where heat is wanted.

New Mexico Red - These peppers are a rusty red. They are commonly used in making chili powder and enchilada sauces. They have a nutty flavor and are a little hot.

Pasilla - This pepper is a small dark pepper that is very fragrant. It is hot and is used in chili powders and making chili.

Ancho - This is the dried version of the poblano. It is dark and wrinkled and has a rich smell. This is the pepper beloved by Texans for making Tex-Mex chili sauces and stews.

Pequins or Piquins - A small red pepper that is used mostly for the heat as it is very hot but has little flavor. It is a traditional flavoring in the Mexican sausage, chorizo.

Chipotle - This is the dried, smoked version of a ripe jalapeño. When added to soups and stews, it adds a rich smoky flavor.

Cayenne - This is usually used in the powdered form and is prized for its heat. This pepper looks similar to the Chile de Arbol pepper.

Food Products Used in This Cookbook

Rotel® Tomatoes - A brand of canned tomatoes with hot green chiles, commonly used in Tex-Mex cooking.

Goya Sazón® - Seasoning packets contain achiote and dried cilantro. It gives a pleasing orange color to your dish. This seasoning is found in the Mexican food section.

Fritos® - A brand of corn chips that have been long popular in Texas cooking.

Chili Beans - Pinto beans cooked in a chili sauce. Ranch Style® beans are the most popular of the canned chili beans.

Picante Sauce - Bottled tomato salsa, Pace® is a popular brand.

Appetizers and Snacking Stuff

New Mexico green chile

You will need something to snack on while your chili simmers on the stove. These appetizer recipes are mostly Southwestern with flavors that go well with chili.

Artichoke and Green Chile Dip

1 (14-ounce) can artichoke hearts
1 cup mayonnaise
3 pickled jalapeño slices, minced
1 (4-ounce) can chopped green chiles

1 cup grated fresh Parmesan cheese
Tortilla chips, bagel chips or
　　French bread slices

Heat oven to 400 degrees. Drain artichoke hearts well and chop fine. Mix all ingredients together and place in shallow buttered baking or pie dish. Place in hot oven for 20 minutes or until bubbling. Serve at once with tortilla chips, bagel chips or French bread slices. Makes 6 servings.

Best Guacamole Dip

3 large avocados
1 ripe tomato, chopped
6 pieces of bacon, fried crisp and drained
1/2 onion, minced
1 teaspoon garlic powder

1 (4-ounce) can chopped green chiles
Juice of 1/2 a lime
1 teaspoon salt
1 bag of tortilla chips

Chile peppers

Peel avocados and place in bowl with tomato; mash with fork, leaving some lumps. Crumble bacon and add to avocado mixture. Add other ingredients and mix well. Place in refrigerator for 20 to 30 minutes before serving. Serve with tortilla chips. Makes 6 to 8 servings.

Cheese Straws

1 cup grated sharp Cheddar cheese
1/2 cup butter
1 cup flour
1 egg yolk

1/2 teaspoon salt
1/2 teaspoon cayenne pepper
Paprika

Mix all ingredients together, except paprika, to make a stiff dough. Chill the dough for at least one hour. Roll out dough on floured board to about 1/8" thick. Cut into strips, 2" long and 1/2" wide. Bake on cookie sheet in a 400-degree oven for 10 minutes. Sprinkle with paprika when removed from cookie sheet. Let cool on wire rack. Makes about 75 cheese straws. Store in airtight container and they will keep for several weeks.

Cold Chile con Queso

1 pint small curd cottage cheese
1 (4-ounce) can chopped green chiles
2 tablespoons chopped jalapeño
  pickle slices

1 small ripe tomato, chopped
1 avocado, chopped
1 tablespoon finely chopped onion
1 bag of tortilla chips

Mix all ingredients "except chips"
together well. Serve immediately
with tortilla chips. Serves 6 to 8.

Left and right, jalapeño peppers

Easy Taco Dip

1 (16-ounce) can refried beans
1/3 cup picante sauce
1 pound lean ground beef
1 package taco seasoning mix
1 cup grated Longhorn Cheddar cheese
1 cup sour cream

1/2 cup chopped green onions
1 ripe tomato, diced
1 (3-ounce) can sliced black olives, drained
1 avocado, peeled and diced
1 bag of tortilla chips

Mix refried beans with picante sauce and spread mixture in 1-1/2 quart baking dish. Brown ground beef, add taco seasoning and cook according to package directions. Spread meat mixture evenly over refried beans. Sprinkle with Cheddar cheese and ripe olives. Bake in a 350-degree oven for 15 to 20 minutes. Spoon sour cream on top. Sprinkle the chopped green onion, chopped tomato, olives, and diced avocado evenly on top and serve immediately with corn tortilla chips. Makes 6 to 8 servings.

Jalapeño Sausage Balls

A baker's dozen of jalapeño peppers

3-1/4 cups Bisquick® or other biscuit mix
1 pound bulk sausage (uncooked)

12 ounces sharp Cheddar cheese, grated
4 pickled jalapeños, finely chopped

Blend ingredients together. Roll into small size balls and place on parchment paper lined or greased cookie sheet. Bake at 375 degrees for 20 minutes or until brown. Makes 50 to 60 balls.

Navajo Tacos

This snack is made with fry bread instead of tortillas and is popular in Arizona and New Mexico. Traditional fry bread is made in large disks and the Navajo taco eaten with a fork. The recipe for fry bread is in the bread and rolls section of this cookbook.

8 fry bread disks, freshly made
2 cups refried beans
3 cups cooked pork or chicken
1 cup taco sauce

1 cup shredded lettuce
2 tomatoes, chopped
2 cups grated Cheddar or Monterey
Jack cheese

To make the taco, spread each piece of fry bread with refried beans, sprinkle with chopped chicken or pork, and spoon on a little taco sauce. Sprinkle with shredded lettuce and chopped tomato and top with grated Cheddar or Monterey Jack cheese. Makes 8 servings.

Never-fail Chile con Queso

2 tablespoons oil
1 large onion, chopped
2 cloves garlic, minced
1 (4-ounce) can chopped green chiles

1 (16-ounce) can diced tomatoes
2-1/2 cups grated Velveeta® cheese
1 cup heavy cream
1 bag of tortilla chips

Heat oil in heavy skillet or pan, add onion and cook until onions are limp and clear. Add garlic and cook one minute more. Add other ingredients and cook on low until cheese is melted. Add more cream or milk if too thick. Serve with tortilla chips. Serves 6 to 8.

Ranch-style Oyster Crackers

2 (10-ounce) packages oyster crackers
1 package Hidden Valley® Ranch
  Dressing Mix

1 cup salad oil
1 tablespoon minced dill weed
1 teaspoon black pepper

Mix all ingredients in a large oven-proof dish. Bake in 200-degree oven for 1 hour, stirring every 15 minutes. Makes 8 cups. Store in airtight container.

Texas Crab Grass

2 (8-ounce) blocks cream cheese, softened
1/2 cup sour cream
1 pound chopped cooked crab meat
1/4 cup finely chopped green bell pepper
1/4 cup finely minced onion
1 tablespoon OLD BAY® Seasoning
1 bunch fresh parsley, finely chopped or 1/2 cup dried parsley flakes

Mix cream cheese and sour cream. Add crab meat, bell pepper, minced onion, and OLD BAY® Seasoning, mixing well. Spread in shallow dish. Cover with minced parsley or parsley flakes. Let stand in refrigerator about 30 minutes to chill. Serve with wheat crackers. Serve 10 to 12.

Tex-Mex Bean Dip

2 cans refried beans
1 (4-ounce) can chopped green chiles
2 teaspoons garlic powder
2 tablespoons chili powder
1 tablespoon Tabasco® Sauce

1 teaspoon salt
1 teaspoon black pepper
1-1/2 cups grated Cheddar cheese
1 bag of tortilla chips

Heat refried beans in heavy skillet. Add green chiles and seasonings, mixing well and cooking on low. Add grated cheese and stir until melted. Serve immediately with tortilla chips. Serves 6 to 8.

Spinach con Queso

This is a chile con queso with a difference. For more heat, use Pepper Jack cheese.

1 (10-ounce) bunch fresh spinach or
   1 (10-ounce) box plain frozen spinach
1 tablespoon oil
1/4 cup finely minced onion
1 tablespoon flour

1 (4-ounce) can chopped green chiles
1/2 cup cream or evaporated milk
1 (3-ounce) package cream cheese, cubed
2 cups grated Monterey Jack
   or Pepper Jack cheese

Cook spinach, then finely chop and press all liquid from the spinach. In a heavy sauce pan, heat the oil and add the minced onion and cook until onion is soft

(continued)

Spinach con Queso *(continued)*

and clear, 3 to 4 minutes. Add flour and cook 1 minute more. Add spinach and green chiles, mixing well and cooking for another minute. Add cream and cook until mixture boils, about 1 minute. REDUCE HEAT to low and gradually add the cream cheese, stirring until cheese is melted. Gradually add the Monterey Jack cheese. Do not allow mixture to boil or cheese will separate. Serve at once with tortilla chips. Serves 8.

*An assortment of peppers
(bell, Anaheim, jalapeño and more)*

Stuffed Jalapeños

1 (11-ounce) can whole pickled
  jalapeños
1 (8-ounce) package cream cheese

1/4 cup chopped pecans
Onion powder to taste

Jalapeño peppers

Drain jalapeños and split down side and remove seeds. Mix cream cheese, pecans and onion powder. Stuff each chile with the cheese mixture, press closed and chill for several hours or until firm. Slice jalapeños into bite-size pieces to serve. Jalapeños can be stuffed with tuna or chicken salad or other cheese mixtures. Makes 6 to 8 servings.

Texas-Pecan Pinwheels

1/2 cup finely chopped, toasted
    pecans
1 (8-ounce) package cream cheese
1 teaspoon garlic powder

2 tablespoons picante sauce
1 tablespoon finely chopped jalapeño
4 (8-inch) flour tortillas

To toast pecans, place on baking sheet and bake in a 350-degree oven for 10 to 12 minutes, stirring often. Mix cream cheese, garlic powder, and picante sauce. Add the chopped jalapeños and pecans. Spread about 6 tablespoons of the mixture on each flour tortilla. Roll each tortilla up tight and wrap in plastic wrap. Refrigerate the rolls for at least 4 hours or overnight. To serve, remove wrap and cut into 1/2-inch thick slices. Serves 10 to 12.

Salads, Salsas, and Sandwiches

Here are some recipes to use when you want to add a little something more to your chili meal. A fresh tasting salsa, a crisp salad or a hearty sandwich, all will go well with that bowl of chili. *An assortment of peppers shown at left.*

Corn and Hominy Salad

Here is a colorful and flavorful salad that will brighten any meal.

1 (15-1/2-ounce) can white hominy
1 (15-1/2-ounce) can fresh pack
  yellow corn
1 red bell pepper, seeded and chopped
1/4 cup finely minced onion

1/4 cup chopped cilantro leaves
1/3 cup oil and vinegar dressing:
Olive oil (3 parts)
Vinegar (1 part)
Salt and pepper to taste

Drain and rinse the hominy and corn and place in large bowl. Add other ingredients and mix. Let the salad chill for several hours before serving. Newman's Own® Olive Oil and Vinegar Dressing is good on this or make your own as listed above. Season with salt and pepper. Serves 6 to 8.

Cowboy Cole Slaw

1/2 head of cabbage, thinly shredded
1 red bell pepper, seeded and diced
1 green bell pepper, seeded and diced
1 large carrot, grated
1/2 cup chopped green onion

1/4 cup mayonnaise
1/4 cup sour cream
1 tablespoon garlic powder
1 tablespoon cider vinegar
Salt and pepper to taste

Mix vegetables in large bowl. In smaller bowl, mix a dressing of the mayonnaise, sour cream, garlic powder, and vinegar. Pour over the vegetables and toss to mix. Season with salt and pepper. Refrigerate before serving. Make 6 to 8 servings.

Health Nut Sandwich Spread

2 (8-ounce) packages cream cheese
1 green bell pepper, chopped
1 bunch radishes, finely chopped
1/2 cup chopped pecans

2 carrots, finely chopped
1 bunch green onions, chopped
2 teaspoons Creole seasoning
6 strips bacon, fried crisp and crumbled

Mix all ingredients. Chill about 1 hour. Serve on health-nut bread or 7-grain bread with lettuce, sliced tomatoes, and avocado slices. Serves 4 to 6.

Bell pepper

Hot Cheese and Bacon Toast

This recipe makes delicious little cheese toasts that go well with chili.

8 slices bacon
1/3 cup mayonnaise
1 cup shredded sharp Cheddar cheese
1 small onion, grated
1 egg, lightly beaten

Fresh ground black pepper
1 teaspoon Worcestershire® Sauce
2 dashes Tabasco® Sauce
8 slices white bread

Fry bacon until crisp. Drain on paper towels and set aside. When cool, crumble bacon. In large bowl, combine all ingredients, except the bread, mixing well. Cut crust from bread and toast on both sides. Spread each slice with cheese mixture, then cut into 3 strips. Sprinkle with paprika. Place toast strips on cookie sheet and bake in an oven at 350 degrees for about 15 to 20 minutes or until lightly browned and puffy. Serve hot. Makes 4 to 6 servings.

Grilled Corn and Pineapple Salsa

1 small pineapple, cleaned and cut
    into disks
1 red bell pepper
1/4 red onion
1 ear of corn

1 fresh jalapeño pepper
1 tablespoon chopped cilantro
1/4 cup extra-virgin olive oil
Juice of 1 lime
Pinch of salt

Bell pepper

Grill pineapple, red pepper and onion, then dice. Grill corn and cut kernels from cob. Grill jalapeño and slice, removing seeds and membrane. Mix with other ingredients, tossing to blend well. Season with salt and pepper. Serves 4 to 6.

Jicama Salad

Jicama is a root vegetable that tastes like a cross between an apple and a potato. It goes well in salads and the Spanish prounciation is "hick-a-ma."

1/2 small jicama, peeled
1/2 red bell pepper, seeds and
    membranes removed
1/2 yellow bell pepper, seeds and
    membranes removed
1/2 carrot
1/2 zucchini, only part that has
    green skin attached

Dressing:
4 tablespoons virgin olive oil
2 tablespoons lime juice
1/2 teaspoon cayenne pepper
Salt to taste

Bell pepper.

Cut all vegetables into thin julienne strips and place in bowl with dressing and toss to mix. Makes 6 to 8 servings.

Nopalitos Salad

Here's a salad made of the leaves of the prickly pear cactus. The *nopalitos* are available in Mexican grocery stores.

1 (16-ounce) jar plain *nopalitos,* drained
2 green onions, chopped
2 teaspoons chopped cilantro

1 ripe tomato diced
2 tablespoons green chiles, diced
2 tablespoons grated Parmesan cheese
1/3 cup oil and vinegar dressing

Combine all ingredients and toss to mix. Chill several hours before serving. Serves 6.

Mango Salsa

2 large ripe mangos, peeled
  and diced
1/2 onion, finely chopped
1/2 red bell pepper, finely chopped

2 serrano peppers, diced
Juice of 1 lime
2 tablespoons finely chopped cilantro
1 teaspoon salt

 Mix all ingredients and let stand for a least 30 minutes before serving. Serves 6.

Old South Pimiento Cheese

This sandwich spread brings back memories of Grandmother's bridge parties and tall glasses of iced tea. A pimiento cheese sandwich is a perfect companion to a bowl of chili.

8 ounces Longhorn Cheddar cheese
1 (4-ounce) jar diced pimientos, undrained
1/2 cup mayonnaise

2 tablespoons wine vinegar
Fresh ground black pepper to taste
2 tablespoons sweet pickle relish (optional)

Grate cheese in large bowl; add other ingredients, mixing well. Chill an hour or so before using. Makes enough spread for 5 to 6 sandwiches.

Salsa Fresca (Fresh Table Sauce)

Red ripe tomatoes are a must for this salsa. If you buy unripe tomatoes, leave them out on the counter or windowsill and they will continue to ripen.

4 ripe Roma or plum tomatoes
2 fresh jalapeños, minced
1 clove garlic, finely minced
1/2 small onion, finely chopped

1 tablespoon oil
1/2 teaspoon salt
1 tablespoon cider vinegar or
    freshly squeezed lime juice

Chop tomatoes into small pieces. Place all ingredients in food processor or blender and process briefly. Let stand in refrigerator for 30 minutes before serving. Makes 1-1/2 cups.

Tortas

Contrary to belief, Mexican food is more than tacos and tortillas. This Mexican classic sandwich calls for using *bolillos,* a torpedo-shaped roll sold in Mexican grocery stores and bakeries. French bread rolls can be substituted.

6 Mexican rolls *(bolillos)* or
   French rolls
1 cup refried beans
6 slices ham

6 slices cheese (American or Cheddar)
1 cup guacamole (p. 15)
Salsa

Split rolls in half. Spread refried beans on one side of each roll; lay on slices of ham and cheese. Place rolls under broiler until cheese melts and rolls are lightly toasted. Top with guacamole and pass the salsa. Makes 6 servings.

Meat Lovers' Chili

Hot red pepper

Many chili lovers will turn their noses up at a chili dish that does not have chunks of beef in the bowl. All the recipes in this section have meat.

B & B Chili (Beef and Beans)

1 pound black beans	1 teaspoon salt
3 cups chicken broth	2 tablespoons garlic powder
2 pounds ground beef	1 (10-ounce) can Rotel® tomatoes
2 tablespoons oil	2 tablespoon flour
6 tablespoons chili powder	Rice (2 to 3 cups prepared)
2 tablespoons oil	1/2 cup onion, chopped

Wash black beans and place in pot with chicken broth. Bring to a boil and reduce to simmer, let cook for 1 hour. Brown meat in oil and add to beans. Add remaining ingredients and cook for 2 more hours until beans are soft, adding water or chicken broth as needed. Serve with rice and chopped onion. Serves 4 to 6.

Boot Dog Chili

I named this recipe for my little tan dog, Buddy. He showed up at our house one hot summer day when we were photographing cowboy boots. He adopted us on the spot and has been my constant companion ever since. He still likes to go outside when we photograph-and he loves it when I add a little chili to his dog food.

3 pounds beef chuck, trimmed, and cut into cubes
3 medium onions, chopped
1 green bell pepper, chopped
2 jalapeños, seeded and chopped
4 cloves garlic, minced
1/2 teaspoon oregano
1 teaspoon ground cumin
1 (8-ounce) can tomato sauce
1 (10-ounce) can Rotel® tomatoes
4 cups water
3 tablespoons chili powder

Brown meat in heavy pan. Add other ingredients and simmer for 1-1/2 to 2 hours. Taste and add salt and pepper as needed. To improve flavor, chill overnight and reheat the next day. Serves 6 to 8.

Bubba's Chili

Everyone in Texas knows a Bubba. He's the good ol' boy in a cowboy hat driving a pick-up truck with a rifle in the back window and a cooler on the floorboard.

3 pounds coarse ground beef
3 onions, chopped
4 cloves garlic, minced
6 tablespoons chili powder
2 teaspoons cayenne pepper
1 tablespoon sweet paprika
2 teaspoons ground cumin

1 teaspoon dried oregano
2 (8-ounce) cans tomato sauce
2 (10-ounce) can Rotel® tomatoes
1 packet Goya Sazón® Seasoning
1 (16-ounce) can kidney beans
2 tablespoons Tabasco® Sauce
6 pack of beer

Dried red chile peppers, tied into a chile ristra

Brown meat in a heavy skillet. Add onions and minced garlic, cooking until onions are limp. Add chili powder, cayenne pepper, paprika, cumin, and oregano and mix well, cooking another minute or two. Add tomato sauce, Rotel® tomatoes, Sazón® Seasoning, kidney beans, Tabasco® Sauce and 1 can of the beer. Season to taste with salt and pepper. Bring to a boil, lower heat and cook on low until done. As the chili cooks, drink the remaining beer. The longer the chili cooks and the more beer you drink, the better the chili will taste. Serves 6 to 8. Please cook and drive responsibly.

Cactus Chili

This recipe calls for *nopalitos,* the tender young pads of the prickly pear cactus. *Nopalitos* are sold in jars in the Mexican food section at the supermarket.

2 tablespoons oil
1-1/2 pounds chuck beef cut into
   1/2-inch cubes
1 large onion, chopped
3 cloves garlic, minced
4 tablespoons chili powder
1 teaspoon ground cumin
1 teaspoon Mexican oregano

1 teaspoon cayenne pepper
1 tablespoon paprika
1 (12-ounce) can Rotel® tomatoes
1 cup tomato juice
1 bottle dark Mexican beer
1 (15-ounce) can chili beans
1 (10-ounce) jar *nopalitos*
Salt and pepper to taste

Heat oil in large cast iron skillet. Brown meat cubes, adding onions and cook a few minutes more. Add garlic and cook until aroma is released (about 1 minute). Add seasonings and mix well. Add the *Anaheim pepper* Rotel® tomatoes, tomato juice and beer. Simmer on low for 1 to 1-1/2 hours or until meat is tender. Add more liquid if needed. Drain *nopalitos* and beans and add to chili. Correct the seasoning and simmer fifteen minutes more. Serve with fresh chopped cilantro and sour cream for garnish. Pass the tortilla chips. Makes 4 to 6 servings.

Chicken and Rice Chili

Here's an easy recipe with a Caribbean taste.

Dried ancho chile pods shown at left and right

4 chicken breast halves
Salt and pepper to taste
2 tablespoons oil
1 cup rice
1 large onion, chopped
4 cloves garlic, minced

2 to 3 tablespoons ground ancho chile powder (Spice Island® or McCormick®)
1 (15-1/2-ounce) can black beans, drained
2 cups reserved chicken broth
1 cup tomato salsa

Season chicken breast with salt and pepper, place in pan. Barely cover with water

and cook until done, about 20 minutes. When cool, dice meat and set aside. Reserve the chicken broth. Heat oil in heavy pan and add rice and cook until lightly browned. Add onions and garlic and cook until onions are clear. Add chicken and the ancho chile powder, mixing well. Add

Six dried ancho chile pods beans and chicken broth and simmer uncovered on low until rice is cooked, about 30 minutes, adding more chicken broth as needed. Stir in tomato salsa and cook five minutes more. Adjust seasoning and serve with chopped avocado, chopped green onions, and sour cream thinned with a little lime juice with tortilla chips on the side. Serves 4.

Chili Brick

This is an old recipe that goes back to when chili would be formed into "bricks." The chili brick would be reheated to serve, adding liquid as needed. Chili bricks were so popular that they were commercially made and sold at grocery stores.

2 to 3 pounds suet, coarsely ground
10 pounds coarsely ground beef
3 tablespoons salt
1 tablespoon sugar
1 (1/4-ounce) can chili powder or
   1-1/8 tablespoons chili powder

1 ounce ground cumin
Pinch of oregano
1 can kidney beans
1 large can tomato juice or water

Use a large heavy kettle. Melt 2 to 3 pounds suet that has been coarsely ground.

Add 10 pounds coarsely ground beef (this coarse grind used to be called chili-grind). Cook beef 5 to 10 minutes. Add 3 tablespoons salt and 1 tablespoon sugar. Cook about 30 minutes. Add 1/4-ounce can chili powder, 1 ounce ground cumin and a pinch of oregano. Cook 5 minutes longer, stirring constantly. Pour into pans or molds and cool. Cut into squares and refrigerate or freeze. Reheat as needed. If you add beans when reheating also add some tomato juice or water. Makes 3 to 4 chili bricks.

Jalapeño peppers

Chile con Carne – 1906

This recipe comes from a cookbook, *101 Mexican Dishes,* published in 1906. You can see by reading the recipe that the way of preparing chili has changed.

1 pound pork
5 chiles
2 garlic cloves
Dash of black pepper

1 tomato, cooked
Lard or vegetable oil
Dash of salt

Cut a pound of pork into inch chunks and parboil. Soak five chiles in hot water, take out the seeds and veins, wash them well and put in a mortar. Pound the chiles to a pulp then add the black pepper, garlic, and a cooked tomato. Fry this in hot lard; then add the meat with some of the liquid in which it was boiled and a little salt. Cover and let it cook down until rather thick.

Chile con Carne Mole

To make your own mole takes all day and calls for 25 to 30 ingredients. Lucky for us cooks, commercial mole is sold in the Mexican food section at the supermarket.

2 tablespoons oil
1-1/2 pounds cooked chicken or
   turkey
1 onion, chopped
1 clove garlic, chopped
2 tablespoons chili powder
5 cups chicken or turkey stock

4 tablespoons mole
1 (16-ounce) can tomato purée
2 tablespoons cocoa
2 tablespoons wine vinegar
3 tablespoons flour
Salt and pepper to taste

(continued)

Chile con Carne Mole   *(continued)*

Sour cream
Chopped avocado

4 corn tortillas, cut in thin strips and
fried until crisp

Heat oil in heavy pan, then place meat in pan. Add onions, cooking until translucent; add garlic and cook a minute or two more. Add chili powder, mixing well; add stock, mole, tomato purée, cocoa, and wine vinegar and simmer for 45 minutes, adding more stock or water as needed. In a small bowl, mix enough water with the flour to make a runny paste and stir into the chili. Let simmer five minutes more to thicken. Add salt and pepper as needed. Serve garnished with the sour cream, avocado and corn tortilla strips. Serves 4 to 6.

Chili Pasilla

The dark, almost black pasilla chile is found in most Mexican food markets. It has more heat than jalapeños and anchos.

5 to 6 pasilla chiles
3 garlic cloves, chopped
1 teaspoon ground cumin
1 quart *tomatillos,* husk removed,
   halved and divided

1 pound round steak
1/3 cup flour
2 tablespoons oil
1 teaspoon black pepper
Salt to taste

Cut off stems and remove seeds from pasilla chiles. Cover with boiling water and

(continued)

Chili Pasilla   *(continued)*

let stand for 15 to 20 minutes to soften. Remove chiles from soaking water, reserving the liquid. Place softened chiles in blender or food processor. Add garlic, cumin, and half the *tomatillos,* which have been halved, and process until smooth. Add the remaining *tomatillos* and process until smooth. Cut steak into 1-inch cubes and coat with flour. Brown in hot oil. Add 2 to 3 tablespoons of the flour and cook until flour is browned. Add the chile purée and simmer on low until meat is tender, about 30 minutes. Add liquid from chiles as needed. Taste and season with more salt and pepper as needed. Serve with chopped onion and flour tortillas. Serves 4.

Chipotle Chili

2 tablespoons oil
2 pounds lean ground beef
2 large onions, chopped
3 tablespoons chili powder
2 tablespoons ground cumin
1-1/2 tablespoons garlic powder

2 tablespoons canned minced chipotle
  with adobo sauce
2 tablespoons adobo sauce
Salt and pepper to taste
3 cups water
1/2 cup chopped cilantro, divided

In heavy skillet or Dutch oven, heat the oil and sauté the meat and onion until

(continued)

Chipotle Chili   *(continued)*

beef is cooked, about 10 minutes. Add the chili powder, cumin, garlic powder, chipotle, and adobo sauce and cook a few minutes more. Add the water, salt, pepper, and half of the cilantro. Cook on low for about 1-1/2 hours, add water as needed. In the last 15 minutes of cooking, add remaining cilantro and adjust the seasoning. Garnish with grated Cheddar cheese, chopped onion, and sour cream. Serves 4 to 6.

Bell and jalapeño peppers

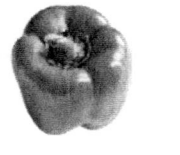

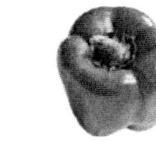

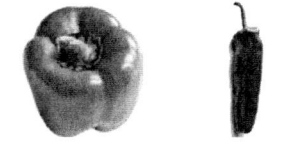

Chorizo Chili

This recipe calls for two popular South Texas ingredients, chorizo and chile pequin.

1 tablespoon bacon drippings or oil
1 pound chorizo (Mexican sausage)
1 tablespoon chile pequin, crushed
2 tablespoons chili powder
2 cloves garlic, minced
1 teaspoon dried oregano
1/4 teaspoon coriander

2 tablespoons flour
1 (15-ounce) can crushed tomatoes
1 tablespoon vinegar
Salt to taste
2 cups cooked pinto beans
2 to 3 cups water or stock

(continued)

Chorizo Chili *(continued)*

Heat oil in heavy pan; crumble chorizo and brown in oil. Add crushed chile pequin, chili powder, garlic, oregano, and coriander, stirring well. Add flour, tomatoes, and vinegar and let simmer a few minutes. Add beans and 2 cups water or stock and simmer for 45 minutes, adding more liquid as needed. Serve with flour tortillas. Serves 4 to 6.

Habañero pepper (top), jalapeño peppers (bottom)

Classic Bowl of Red

Here's what it is all about, a classic bowl of red chili with the rich flavor of ancho chiles. A little more work, but well worth the effort.

6 ancho chiles, stems and seeds removed
2 cloves garlic
1 tablespoon rice wine vinegar
1 teaspoon salt
2 tablespoons oil or bacon drippings
2 pounds stew meat, cut in 1/2" cubes
1 tablespoon paprika
1 tablespoon ground cumin
1 teaspoon cayenne pepper
3 tablespoons masa harina

Place ancho chiles in bowl and cover with boiling water. Let stand 20 minutes.

(continued)

Classic Bowl of Red *(continued)*

Remove the anchos and place in blender or food processor. Add garlic, vinegar, and salt and enough of the soaking water to make a thin paste when blended. Set aside when done.

Six dried ancho chile pods

Heat oil or bacon drippings in heavy skillet. Brown the meat in oil. Add the chile paste, paprika, ground cumin, and cayenne pepper. Add enough water to cover and simmer on low until meat is tender (1 to 2 hours). To thicken the chili, make a thin gruel with the masa harina and water and add to chili, mixing well. Let cook for another 20 minutes. Making chili a day ahead of serving improves the flavor. Serves 4 to 6.

Cook-Off Chili

A new layer of zaniest was added to chili culture when the first chili cook-off was held in Terlingua, Texas in 1967. Since then, chili cook-offs have become a popular weekend event to raise funds for charities, consume larger quantities of beer and have an over-all good time.

3-1/2 to 4 pounds beef chuck
 trimmed and cut into 1/2-inch pieces
Salt and pepper to taste
4 tablespoons oil
4 onions, chopped
4 cloves garlic, finely chopped
1 (6-ounce) can tomato paste
2 (8-ounce) cans tomato sauce

4 tablespoons chili powder
2 teaspoons cayenne pepper
3 tablespoons oregano
2 tablespoons paprika
1 tablespoon Tabasco® Sauce
2 teaspoons ground cumin
5 cups water
1/4 cup masa harina   *(continued)*

Cook-Off Chili   *(continued)*

Season meat with salt and pepper to taste. Heat oil in heavy Dutch oven or iron skillet and add meat in several batches, browning each batch well. Set meat aside and brown onions and garlic in oil, cooking until onions are limp. Return meat to skillet and add tomato paste and tomato sauce; bring to a boil and add chili powder, cayenne pepper, oregano, paprika, Tabasco® Sauce, and cumin, mixing well. Add 5 cups of water and bring to a boil, then lower heat, and cover and simmer for 2 to 3 hours or until meat is tender. Add more water if needed. Taste and correct the seasoning. Mix the masa harina with a little water to make a thin runny paste and stir into the chili. Let cook for about 15 more minutes, stirring until thickened. It is then ready to serve. Chilling overnight and reheating improves the chili's flavor. Makes 6 servings.

Curried Pepper and Pork Stir Fry
by Mary Ann Reiter

1/4 cup of canola oil, divided
1 teaspoon salt
1 pound of pork loin cut into
   1/2-inch by 1/2-inch by 3-inch strips
4 to 6 bell peppers, preferably various
   colors, cut into strips

2 large onions cut into strips
4 to 6 tablespoons curry powder
   (I like to use Spice Island® brand)
1-1/4 cups chicken broth
Juice from 1/2 a lemon
1 tablespoon cornstarch

Heat a large heavy wok. When hot, add half of the oil. Add the salt and pork stir frying until it loses the pink color. Remove the meat from the wok. Add the remaining oil to the wok along with the peppers and onions, stir frying until

(continued)

Curried Pepper and Pork Stir Fry *(continued)*

softened. Lower the heat slightly and add the curry powder. The amount of curry powder will depend on the degree of hotness desired. Stir fry for 2 or 3 minutes to cook the curry powder. Add the stock and lemon juice; cook stirring frequently until the sauce thickens and is clear. Return the pork to the pan, stir in the meat, heat and serve over rice or noodles.

Bell peppers

Mama's Saturday Chili

I remember my mother cooking a big pot of chili on the stove every Saturday. All six of us kids looked forward to that chili.

1 pound coarse-ground pork
2 pounds coarse-ground beef
1 large onion, chopped
2 cloves garlic, chopped
4 tablespoons Gebhardt's® Chili Powder
2 tablespoons pure ground chile

3 teaspoons ground cumin
1 teaspoon Mexican oregano
1 (16-ounce) can crushed tomatoes
1-1/2 cups beef broth, divided
Optional: 2 cups cooked *frijoles* (pinto beans)

(continued)

Mama's Saturday Chili   *(continued)*

Brown pork, beef, onion, and garlic. Cook until meat is browned and onions are limp. Add both chili powders, cumin, and oregano, mixing well. Add tomatoes and some of the beef broth. Lower heat and simmer for 1 hour, adding more broth as needed. Add beans and cook 15 minutes more. This chili is better when served the next day. Serves 6 without beans; 8 with beans.

Mashed Potatoes and Chili Variation

A tradition of adding mashed potatoes on top of any mild chili recipe is how chili is served in Mary Lou Hattery's family. Mary Lou* said adding mashed potatoes dates back to her childhood. This custom appears to have originated in the Wisconsin and Michigan areas. Others have heard of chili being added on top of mashed potatoes in the bottom of the bowl. Combining mashed potatoes with buttermilk before serving with a bowl of chili is another favorite variation.

*Mary Lou, is an excellent resource for Penfield Books and compiled our *French Recipes* title.

Official State Fair of Texas Chili (1952)

Long before chili cook-offs, a chili recipe contest was held at the State Fair of Texas. In 1952, a total of 55 people submitted their entries. Mrs. V. F. Ventura won the contest and held the title for over fifteen years. In her recipe, she calls for a small 1-ounce bottle of chili powder which is no longer sold. This would be equal to 4-1/2 tablespoons of chili powder.

2 pounds ground beef
4 tablespoons chopped garlic
1 teaspoon shortening
1 small bottle chili powder or
   4-1/2 tablespoons chili powder

2 tablespoons flour
2 teaspoons ground cumin seed
3 cups water
1 teaspoon salt
1/4 teaspoon black pepper

(continued)

Official State Fair of Texas Chili *(continued)*

Drop ground beef and garlic in hot grease. Cook slowly for 15 minutes. Add chili powder, flour, and cumin seed. Stir and add water, salt and pepper and cook for 35 minutes. Serves 6.

Assortment of jalapeño, bell, Anaheim, and New Mexico peppers and more

Poblano and Chicken Chili

The green poblano is one of my favorite chile peppers. I like to use it in chili and stew. The skin must be removed before using.

3 tablespoons olive oil
1 large onion, chopped
3 poblano peppers, seeded and chopped
3 cloves garlic, minced
1 (16-ounce) can tomatoes
2 tablespoons chili powder
1/2 teaspoon cumin
1 tablespoon chopped fresh cilantro

Salt and pepper to taste
1 (16-ounce) can kidney beans, drained
10 to 12 ounces grilled chicken breast cut into small pieces
2 cups chicken stock
1 tablespoon tomato paste
Chopped green onions
Grated Monterey Jack cheese

(continued)

Poblano and Chicken Chili *(continued)*

Heat oil in heavy pan, add onion and poblano peppers and cook until soft (about 5 minutes). Add the garlic and cook a few minutes more. Add tomatoes, chili powder, cumin, and fresh cilantro. Add salt and pepper, kidney beans, chicken,

Poblano peppers

chicken stock, and tomato paste. Cover and simmer on low about 30 to 40 minutes. Taste and adjust the seasoning. Serve hot with chopped green onions and Monterey Jack cheese as garnish. Makes 4 servings.

Prize-winning Chili

Here's a fiery championship recipe, sure to please your "chili-head" friends.

2 tablespoons oil
1 pound boneless stew meat
1 medium onion, chopped
1 garlic clove, chopped
1/3 cup chili powder

1/2 teaspoon salt
1/2 teaspoon black pepper
1-1/2 teaspoons cumin
1 (8-ounce) can tomato sauce
1-1/2 cups water

Cut meat into small pieces. In heavy pan, heat oil and add meat, cooking until well browned. Remove meat from pan and add onion, garlic, chili powder, salt, pepper, and cumin. Cook until the onion is tender. Return meat to the pan and stir in tomato sauce and water. Bring to boil, then lower heat and simmer for 1 to 1-1/2 hours or until meat is tender, adding more water if needed. Season as needed. Serves 4.

Quick Turkey Chili

An easy recipe given to me by my daughter, Judy. She cooks it up in nothing flat.

1 tablespoon oil
1 pound ground turkey breast
1 large onion, chopped
1 clove garlic, minced

1 package McCormick's® Traditional Chili Seasoning
1 large can Rotel® tomatoes
1 (15-1/2-ounce) can kidney beans
2 cups chicken stock or water

Heat oil in Dutch oven, add turkey and brown. Add onion, garlic, and chili seasoning. Cook until onions are clear. Add tomatoes and kidney beans, mixing well. Add water and bring to boil. Turn to low and cook for 30 minutes or until done. Serve with sour cream, grated cheese, and chips. Serves 4.

Secret Ingredient Chili

A well kept secret known to the ancient Aztecs was that chiles and chocolate go well together.

3 pounds lean ground beef
2 onions, chopped
4 cloves garlic, chopped
1 (16-ounce) can chopped tomatoes
1 (10-ounce) can tomatoes with green chiles
2 (9-ounce) cans tomato sauce
1 teaspoon cumin
1 teaspoon paprika

2 to 3 tablespoons chili powder
2 tablespoons pure chile powder
1 square semi-sweet chocolate
1 can dark beer
1 tablespoon sugar
1 teaspoon cayenne pepper
2 to 3 pickled jalapeños, chopped
Salt and pepper to taste
3 cups water *(continued)*

Secret Ingredient Chili   *(continued)*

Brown meat, onions, and garlic in heavy skillet. Add tomatoes and tomato sauce. Add other ingredients. Cook uncovered over low heat for 2 to 3 hours adding more water if needed. Makes 6 to 8 servings.

Wreath of chile peppers   *Jalapeño peppers*   *Dried arbol peppers*

Venison Chili

This is an old recipe that I have had around for many years. I have also used moose meat when making this chili.

2 tablespoons oil
2 pounds finely chopped venison
4 tablespoons chili powder
1 teaspoon salt
2 teaspoons pepper
1 (46-ounce) can V8® Vegetable Juice

1 large onion, chopped
2 teaspoons garlic powder
2 teaspoons ground cumin
2 medium potatoes, peeled and diced
1 (16-ounce) can chili beans

Heat 2 tablespoons oil in large pot and cook until the venison is browned. Add
(continued)

Venison Chili *(continued)*

Jalapeño peppers

chili powder, salt, and pepper and cook a little longer to dissolve the chili powder. Add V8® juice, onion, garlic powder, cumin, and potatoes and simmer on low for 2 to 3 hours or until meat is tender. Add chili beans and cook for 15 minutes longer. Let stand 5 minutes before serving. Serve with crackers, cheese, and celery sticks. Makes 6 to 8 servings.

White Meat Chili

White chili sounds so exotic, but it is easy to make and tastes great.

6 boneless chicken breast halves
6 cups water
1 teaspoon salt, divided
Pepper to taste
1 pound white beans,
   soaked overnight

4 cloves garlic, chopped, divided
2 onions chopped, divided
2 (4-ounce) cans chopped green chiles
2 teaspoons cumin
2 teaspoons dried oregano

Cook the chicken breasts in the water seasoned with salt and pepper. Cook 20 to 30 minutes until meat is done. Remove chicken from broth and cut into bite size pieces. Reserve the chicken broth. Refrigerate chicken for later use. *(continued)*

White Meat Chili   *(continued)*

Drain the white beans and add to chicken stock. Add 1/2 the garlic, 1/2 the onions, and salt. Bring to a boil, then reduce heat, cover and simmer for 1-1/2 hours or until beans are done, adding water as needed.

Heat a little oil in skillet, sauté remaining onion and garlic, adding green chiles, cumin, oregano, and chicken. Cook for about 5 minutes and add to bean mixture, simmer for 20 minutes. Serve with grated Monterey Jack cheese and chopped green onions for garnish. Serves 6. *Green chile peppers*

Chili U. S. A.

Chili was a dish confined to Texas until the Columbian Exposition was held in Chicago in 1893. At the exposition Texas had a "San Antonio Chili Stand" and sold bowls of chili for five cents each. The chili was a huge success. Visitors went back to their homes with stories of the tasty dish. Soon chili making had spread to all the states. Some areas have developed their own special chili recipes. Here is a sampling of recipes from many areas of the U. S. A.

Arizona Chili

Carne seca or dried beef is a popular meat in Arizona. The jerky is pounded and shredded for use in meat dishes. Here is a chili recipe using *carne seca.*

1 pound beef jerky *(carne seca)*, pounded and shredded	2 tablespoons pure red chile powder
4 tablespoons oil	2 cloves garlic, minced
3 tablespoons flour	1/2 teaspoon dried oregano
	2 cups hot water

Fry pounded, shredded jerky in oil, add flour, chile powder, garlic, and oregano. Simmer for 5 minutes. Add the hot water and simmer for 30 to 45 minutes. Serve with warm tortillas. Makes 4 servings.

Black Hills Chili

Here's a recipe from the Black Hills of South Dakota. I would love to be eating this chili while admiring the beautiful landscape in that area.

2 whole boneless chicken breasts
2 onions, chopped
2 teaspoons garlic powder
2 (8-ounce) cans tomato sauce
1/2 can beer
1-1/2 cups chicken broth
2 tablespoons pure chile powder
2 teaspoons ground cumin
1 teaspoon dried oregano

1 teaspoon soy sauce
1 tablespoon Worcestershire® Sauce
1 teaspoon salt
1 teaspoon paprika
1/2 teaspoon cayenne pepper
1/4 teaspoon dried thyme
1/8 teaspoon dried mustard
Salt and pepper to taste

(continued)

Black Hills Chili *(continued)*

Red chile peppers are dried and ground into cayenne pepper. Many claim this pepper has tremendous health benefits.

Cook chicken breast in water just to cover, seasoned with salt for 30 minutes or until done. Allow chicken to cool, reserving the chicken broth. Chop chicken into small bites. Place chicken in heavy pan along with onions, garlic powder, tomato sauce, beer, chicken broth, and all the seasonings. Bring to a boil, lower heat and simmer covered for about 45 minutes. Add more chicken broth as needed. Taste and correct seasoning. Serves 4 to 6.

In the Himalayan Mountains, the native people of Hunza, have lived for centuries on a diet including apricots and cayenne pepper.

Border Chili

This type of chili is popular along the United States-Mexico border.

2 pounds round steak,
  cubed into small bites
Salt and pepper
1/2 cup flour, divided
3 tablespoons oil
1 onion, chopped
1 (8-ounce) can tomato sauce

1 green bell pepper, chopped
1 (16-ounce) can tomatoes
2 jalapeño peppers, chopped
1 tablespoon chili powder
2 tablespoons cumin
Water as needed

(continued)

Border Chili   *(continued)*

Sprinkle cubed meat with salt and pepper and toss in the flour to coat. Heat oil in heavy pan and fry meat until well browned. Remove meat and cook onions until limp; add two tablespoons flour and stir until browned. Add meat back to pot; add other ingredients and enough water to barely cover. Simmer on low 2 to 3 hours; add a little water as needed. Serve with flour tortillas. Makes 4 to 6 servings.

Bell pepper

Boston Chili Crockpot Style

In Boston, it's all about the beans and go easy on the chili powder.

2 pounds top round beef, cut into
   1/2-inch cubes
1 large onion, chopped
3 cloves garlic, minced
1 (14-ounce) can diced tomatoes
1 (14-ounce) jar roasted red peppers
1 chicken bouillon cube

1 teaspoon cayenne pepper
1 teaspoon chili powder
1 tablespoon cumin
1 tablespoon sweet paprika
1 teaspoon salt
1 teaspoon black pepper
1 (16-ounce) can navy beans, drained

Flour and brown the beef in a little oil. Brown the onions with half the garlic. Place everything in the slow cooker and add about 2 cups water. Cook according to slow cooker instructions, about 4 to 5 hours. Add liquid, if needed. During last hour add the navy beans. Makes 6 to 8 servings.

California Chili

1 pound lean ground beef
1 onion, chopped
2 cloves garlic, chopped
1 (28-ounce) can diced
   tomatoes in purée
1 cup Burgundy wine
Juice of 1 large lemon

4 tablespoons chili powder
1 teaspoon seasoned salt
1 teaspoon black pepper
1/2 teaspoon cayenne pepper
1/2 teaspoon ground cumin
1/2 teaspoon oregano

Brown beef, adding onion and garlic when almost cooked. Continue cooking until onions are clear. Add remaining ingredients and simmer, uncovered for 1 hour. Serves 4.

Cincinnati Three-Way Chili

2 pounds ground sirloin
1 large onion, chopped
3 cloves garlic, minced
3 cups water or stock
3 tablespoons chili powder
1 (1-ounce) square unsweetened
  chocolate, grated
1/2 teaspoon cinnamon

1/4 teaspoon cardamom
1 teaspoon allspice
1/2 teaspoon cumin
1/4 teaspoon cloves
1 (6-ounce) can tomato paste
1/4 cup barbeque sauce
Salt and pepper to taste

In heavy soup pot, place ground beef, onions, and garlic. Cook until meat is browned. Add other ingredients, mixing well. Bring to boil, lower heat and simmer for one hour. Add water as needed. *(continued)*

Cincinnati Three-Way Chili   *(continued)*

For serving, you will need 8 ounces of thin spaghetti, cooked and drained, and 2 cups grated Cheddar cheese. You can also serve with chopped onion and heated kidney beans. Makes 6 to 8 servings.

Note: This Buckeye city has a long tradition of chili parlors serving up their local version of chili. Cincinnati legend says that a Greek immigrant made the original Cincinnati chili to serve over hot dogs. True Cincinnati chili is flavored with chocolate, cinnamon, and cloves. If you request two-way chili, you will get spaghetti with chili on top. Three-way will also have grated cheese. Four-way chili adds chopped onions and five-way chili has beans on the side. And forget the saltines, Cincinnati chili is always served with oyster crackers.

Deep South New Year's Chili

According to Southern tradition, you should eat black-eyed peas on New Year's Day to insure good luck for the coming year. Here is a tasty chili recipe that is a perfect way to start the New Year.

2 pounds ground turkey
2 tablespoons oil
1 large onion, chopped
2 Anaheim green chiles, seeded and chopped
2 fresh jalapeños, chopped
2 teaspoons garlic powder

2 tablespoons chili powder
1 teaspoon cumin
1 (28-ounce) can tomatoes in purée
Salt and pepper to taste
2 cups fresh or frozen black-eyed peas
1 tablespoon Tabasco® Sauce
1 cup cooked rice

(continued)

Deep South New Year's Chili   *(continued)*

In heavy skillet, brown the ground turkey in the oil. Add onion, green chiles, and jalapeño and cook until onions are limp. Add garlic powder, chili powder, and cumin, mixing well. Add tomatoes and salt and pepper to taste. Add a little water as needed. Simmer for 20 minutes; then add the black-eyed peas and Tabasco® Sauce. Simmer another 30 minutes, adding more water as needed. Add the cooked rice and

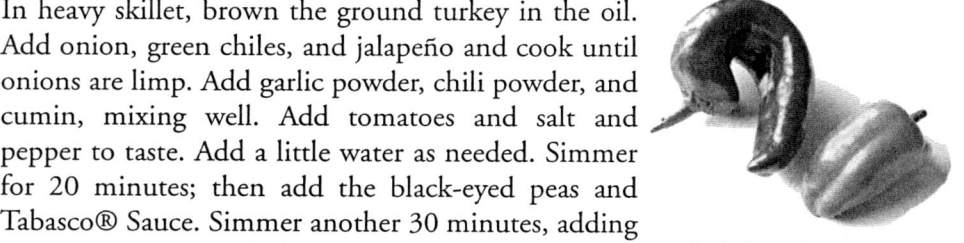

Curled Anaheim pepper

simmer 5 minutes more. Serve with chopped cilantro and diced avocado on top. Jalapeños go well with this dish. Makes 6 to 8 servings.

Hollywood Chili

This recipe is a variation of the famous chili served in Chasen's Restaurant. It was said that this was Clark Gable's favorite chili and that Elizabeth Taylor had a batch flown to her while she was in Italy filming the movie, *Cleopatra*.

8 ounces dry pinto beans
1 (28-ounce) can diced tomatoes
1 large green bell pepper, chopped
2 tablespoons oil
2 large onions, chopped
1/2 cup parsley, chopped
3 cloves garlic, minced

1 pound pork shoulder
2 pounds beef chuck
1/2 cup butter
1/3 cup chili powder
1-1/2 teaspoons ground cumin
1 tablespoon salt
2 teaspoons pepper

(continued)

Hollywood Chili   *(continued)*

Rinse beans and soak in water overnight. The next day, drain off water and place beans in large saucepan and add enough fresh water to barely cover. Bring to boil and cook until soft, 1-1/2 to 2 hours. Add diced tomatoes with the juice and simmer 15 minutes. In a skillet, sauté the bell pepper in the oil for a few minutes. Add the onions and continue cooking until onions are limp. Add the parsley and garlic cooking 2 or 3 minutes more. Add the mixture to the beans. Trim fat from the meat and cut into 1/2-inch cubes. Using same skillet, melt the butter and add the cubed meat. Cook until browned. Drain the meat and add to the bean mixture along with the chili powder, cumin, salt, and pepper. Bring to a boil, cover and reduce heat. Simmer for one hour. Remove cover and cook for 30 minutes longer or until most of the liquid is reduced. The chili should not be runny, but a little thick. Makes 8 to 10 servings. This chili freezes well.

New Mexico *Chili Verde*

Chili verde (green chili) is the most popular type of chili in New Mexico, and it is easy to see why. For a special treat, use Hatch green chiles when they are in season. Hatch chiles can be purchased frozen in some areas.

6 poblano or Hatch green chiles
3 pounds boneless pork butt, cut into
  1-inch pieces
Salt and pepper to taste
1/4 cup flour
3 tablespoons oil
3 large onions, chopped

6 cloves garlic, minced
1 tablespoon dried Mexican oregano
1 tablespoon ground cumin
6 cups chicken stock
1 (16-ounce) can diced tomatoes
  in purée

(continued)

New Mexico *Chili Verde*   (continued)

Poblano peppers

Roast green chiles over a gas flame or under the broiler until the skin is blackened and blistered. Place chiles in paper sack to sweat for about 15 minutes. Remove skin, cut out stems and seeds and chop the chiles into 1-inch pieces. Place diced pork in bowl and season with salt and pepper. Sprinkle flour on meat, tossing to coat well.

Heat the oil in a heavy pan, add meat and cook until browned. Add onions and cook until onions are limp. Add garlic and cook a few minutes longer. Add other ingredients and bring to a boil. Reduce heat and simmer uncovered on low until the meat is tender, about 2 hours, stir often and add more liquid if needed. Taste and adjust the seasoning. Makes 8 to 10 servings.

New York Chili

2 tablespoons oil
4 pounds beef chuck, trimmed and
    cut into bite-sized pieces
2 medium onions, chopped
2 tablespoons garlic powder
2 teaspoons cayenne pepper
4 tablespoons chili powder

1-1/2 teaspoons ground cumin
1 teaspoon oregano
1 (28-ounce) can diced
    tomatoes in purée
1/2 pound ground chuck
Salt and pepper to taste

Heat oil in heavy skillet or soup kettle. Add meat and cook until no longer pink. Add onion and cook until onions are limp. Add garlic powder, cayenne pepper, chili powder, cumin, oregano, and canned tomatoes with purée. Bring to a boil, reduce heat and simmer for 2-1/2 to 3 hours adding water as needed. Add the ground chuck and cook one hour longer. Season with salt and pepper to taste. Serves 6.

Oregon Dungeness Crab and White Bean Chili

1 pound dried cannelloni beans
4 pieces bacon
2 onions, chopped
1 tablespoon garlic powder
2 tablespoons cumin
1/4 cup chopped cilantro
1 (4-ounce) can chopped green chiles
1 tablespoon dried oregano
1 teaspoon cayenne pepper
1 teaspoon ground cloves
1 ham hock or 1 cup ham pieces
8 cups chicken stock
1-1/3 cups grated Monterey Jack cheese
3 cups sour cream
2 pounds Dungeness crab meat, picked over (canned or frozen crab meat can be substituted)
Salt and pepper to taste

Soak beans in water overnight. Next day drain beans. In large heavy pan, fry bacon

Green chile peppers

until crisp, drain on paper towels, reserving bacon drippings. Add onions to bacon drippings and cook until limp. Add garlic powder, cumin, cilantro, green chiles, oregano, cayenne pepper, and cloves. Add drained beans, ham hock, and chicken stock. Cook until beans are tender about 2-1/2 to 3 hours. Remove ham hock and chop meat, returning meat to beans. Keeping heat on low, stir in the cheese and stir until melted. Add sour cream and mix, then add the crab meat and crumble the fried bacon into chili, mixing well, keeping heat on low. Add salt and pepper to taste. Serve topped with croutons and diced avocado. Makes 8 servings.

San Marcus Red Texas Chili

From the 1971 San Marcus, Texas Championship Chili Cook-off. A family favorite.

1 medium onion, chopped	3 tablespoons chili powder
2 garlic cloves, chopped	Salt and pepper to taste
2 pounds coarse ground beef	1 teaspoon whole comino seeds
1 (8-ounce) can tomato sauce	2 teaspoons paprika
1 cup water	Flour to thicken

Brown onions and garlic in bacon drippings. Add meat and cook until grey. Add tomato sauce, water and spices. Bring to a boil, then reduce heat and allow to simmer for at least one hour. To thicken, mix a little flour with water and add to chili, stirring until desired thickness is reached. When ready to serve, you can add pinto beans or for a different treat, try black-eyed peas or hominy. Serves 4. It is better the next day, so make as much as you like and refrigerate or freeze for later.

Springfield "Chilli"

Springfield, Illinois, is proud of their "chilli," please note the extra "l" in the spelling. And in 1993, the Illinois legislature declared Illinois, "The Civilized Chilli Capital of the World." Editor's note: Chillinois style

2 slices bacon
2 medium onions, chopped
3 cloves garlic, minced
2 pounds coarsely ground beef
1 (12-ounce) can beer
  (I recommend Budweiser®)
4 tablespoons chili powder
2 teaspoons Worcestershire® Sauce

1 teaspoon salt
1 teaspoon cumin
1 (15-ounce) can diced tomatoes
  with the juice
1 (8-ounce) can tomato sauce
1 (15-ounce) can pinto beans,
  drained and rinsed

(continued)

Springfield "Chilli" *(continued)*

Fry bacon in heavy pot. Remove bacon and add onions and cook until onions are limp. Add garlic and cook a minute more. Add the beef and stir and cook until beef is browned. Add the beer and cook until reduced to about 1/3 cup liquid. Add chili powder, Worcestershire® Sauce, salt, cumin, diced tomatoes, and tomato sauce. Cover and simmer on low for about 30 minutes. Add the pinto beans and simmer uncovered for 15 minutes more. Serve topped with grated Cheddar cheese, sour cream and chopped green onions with oyster crackers on the side. Makes 6 to 8 servings.

Stillwater Chili

2 pounds ground beef
1 large onion, chopped
1 green bell pepper, chopped
4 tablespoons chili powder
1 tablespoon ground cumin
1 tablespoon garlic powder
1 teaspoon dried oregano

1 (4-ounce) can chopped green chiles
1 (8-ounce) can tomato sauce
1 (10-ounce) can Rotel® tomatoes
1 can chili beans
1/2 teaspoon cayenne pepper
Salt and pepper to taste
2 cups water

Brown meat until it loses its red color. Add onions and bell pepper and continue cooking until onions are limp. Add chili powder, cumin, garlic powder, and

(continued)

Stillwater Chili   *(continued)*

oregano, mixing well and let cook a minute or so. Add
remaining ingredients and simmer on low for 1 to 1-1/2
hours. Add more water as needed. Taste and adjust the
seasoning. Serve with grated Cheddar cheese, chopped
onions, and pickled jalapeños. Serves 4 to 6.

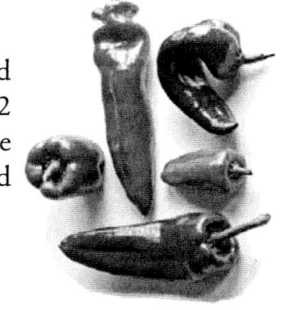

*Jalapeño, Anaheim, and bell
peppers*

Vegetarian Chili

Dried arbol chile pods shown at left and right

Many cooks have discovered that chili tastes great without the meat. Even avowed meat lovers can take to these vegetarian chili dishes.

Lentil Chili

Everyone loves a hearty bowl of lentil soup and these nutritious little legumes make a great chili, too.

4 cups dried lentils, washed in warm water and drained
1 (15-ounce) can tomatoes
2 large onions, chopped
8 cloves garlic, minced
4 tablespoons pure chile powder
2 teaspoons ground cumin
2 teaspoons fresh thyme
2 teaspoons fresh parsley, chopped

1 teaspoon paprika
6 tablespoons tomato paste
2 teaspoons salt
2 teaspoons freshly ground black pepper
2 tablespoons balsamic vinegar
1 teaspoon crushed red pepper flakes
Shredded Cheddar cheese, for garnish

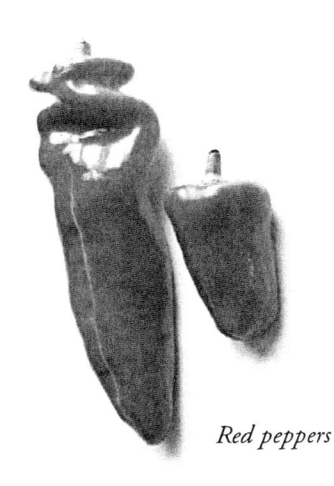

In a large pot, bring lentils and 6 cups of water to boil. Cover and cook for 30 minutes. Stir in tomatoes, onion, garlic, chile powder, cumin, thyme, parsley, and paprika. Partially cover and cook for 1 hour, stirring occasionally and adding water as needed. Stir in tomato paste, salt and pepper and cook 30 minutes longer or until lentils are soft. Stir in balsamic vinegar and red pepper flakes and simmer 10 minutes longer. Top with Cheddar cheese. Serves 6.

Red peppers

Mushroom Chili

2 tablespoons oil
1 large onion, chopped
3 garlic cloves, finely minced
2 teaspoons cumin
3 tablespoons chili powder
1 pound white mushrooms, chopped
1/2 pound shitake mushrooms, chopped

1 pound portobello mushrooms, chopped
1 (16-ounce) can diced tomatoes
1 (16-ounce) can white beans, drained
Salt and pepper to taste
1 small container of sour cream
Fresh cilantro, chopped

Heat oil in heavy pan, add onions and cook until limp. Add minced garlic and cook a few minutes more. Add spices and mushrooms. Cook until mushrooms are soft, about 5 minutes. Add tomatoes, white beans, and one cup of water. Simmer for 20 minutes. Season with salt and pepper. Serve with sour cream and fresh chopped cilantro. Serves 4.

Roasted Veggie Chili

Vegetable oil cooking spray
1 red bell pepper, seeded and diced
1 small eggplant, diced
1 medium onion, cut into eighths
2 medium zucchini, cubed
1 tablespoon olive oil
1 teaspoon each, salt and pepper
2 cloves garlic, minced
1 pound white button mushrooms, quartered

1 bay leaf
1 teaspoon chili powder
1 dried chipotle pepper, stemmed and diced
1 (15-ounce) can white cannelloni beans, drained and rinsed
2 cups vegetable broth or water
1 (16-ounce) can diced tomatoes
2 tablespoons fresh parsley, chopped

(continued)

Roasted Veggie Chili   *(continued)*

Preheat oven to 400 degrees. Coat a baking sheet with cooking spray. In a large bowl, combine the red bell pepper, eggplant, onion, zucchini, oil and salt and pepper, tossing to coat the vegetables. Arrange vegetables on prepared baking sheet in a single layer and roast in oven until almost softened, 25 to 30 minutes, turning occasionally.

In a large Dutch oven or heavy pan, heat a little oil until hot. Add garlic and mushrooms and sauté until mushrooms are soft, about 5 minutes. Add bay leaf, chili powder, chipotle pepper, beans, broth, canned tomatoes, and roasted vegetables. Bring to a boil, then reduce heat and simmer on low for 30 minutes. Add more broth if needed. Stir in parsley and serve hot. Makes 4 to 6 servings.

Vegetarian Black Bean Chili

1 (1-pound) bag black beans
6 cups water
1 (12-ounce) bottle dark beer
3 or 4 tablespoons oil
1 large onion, diced
1 green bell pepper
2 or 3 stalks celery, diced
1 large carrot, chopped
2 zucchinis, diced
1 red bell pepper, diced
1 yellow bell pepper, diced

4 cloves garlic, minced
3 tablespoons wine vinegar
1 bunch Italian parsley, leaves only, chopped
3 or 4 tablespoons chili powder
1 (15-ounce) can yellow corn
1 (15-ounce) can diced tomatoes in purée
Juice of 1 lemon
Salt and pepper to taste

(continued)

Vegetarian Black Bean Chili   *(continued)*

Rinse beans in cold water. Place beans in large soup pot and cover with the 6 cups of water and bottle of beer. Simmer for about 2 to 2-1/2 hours until beans are almost cooked. Add more water as needed. Drain beans, reserving the liquid. Heat oil in large skillet and cook onions, seasoning with salt and pepper. When onions are limp, add green bell pepper, celery and carrots, cooking for five minutes. Add zucchini, red and yellow bell peppers and cook until all vegetables are softened. Add garlic and cook 2 or 3 minutes more. Add 3 cups of the bean liquid, the wine vinegar, chopped parsley and chili powder. Simmer for 30 to 40 minutes. Add corn, tomatoes and black beans. Simmer for 20 to 30 minutes more. Stir in lemon juice and cook 2 or 3 minutes longer. Salt and pepper to taste. Serve in large bowls, sprinkle with more parsley, serve with sour cream, grated Monterey Jack cheese and chopped green onions for toppings. Pass the corn tortilla chips. Makes 6 servings.

Vegetarian Chili

2 tablespoons oil
1 large onion, chopped
2 cloves garlic, minced
3 tablespoons pure chile powder
1 teaspoon oregano
1 teaspoon basil
1 teaspoon ground cumin

2 large zucchini, chopped (2 cups)
2 large carrots, chopped (1 cup)
1 (15-ounce) can chickpeas
1 (15-ounce) can kidney beans
1 (28-ounce) can diced
  tomatoes in purée

Heat oil in large pot, add onion and garlic. Sauté about 5 minutes. Add the seasonings to pot, mixing well. Add zucchini and carrots. Cook at few minutes. Drain the chickpeas and kidney beans then add to pot along with undrained tomatoes. Bring to a boil, reduce heat and simmer for 30 minutes. Add water if needed. Serves 4 to 6.

Vegetarian White Chili

2 tablespoons oil
2 onions, chopped
3 cloves garlic, minced
1 (7-ounce) can chopped green chiles
6 cups water
1 vegetable bouillon cube
1 small can white shoepeg* corn
1 (15-1/2-ounce) can white beans

1 (15-1/2-ounce) can white hominy
2 teaspoons cumin
1 teaspoon white pepper
1 teaspoon dried oregano
1 tablespoon Tabasco® Sauce
1 tablespoon balsamic vinegar
Salt to taste

Shoepeg-A white sweetcorn valued for its sweetness.

Heat oil in skillet, saute onions until clear. Add garlic and chopped green chiles. Cook one minute. Add water and bouillon cube stirring until dissolved. Drain corn, beans, and hominy; add to mixture. Add other ingredients and simmer on low for 45 minutes. Add water if needed. Serve with grated Monterey Jack cheese, sour cream and diced avocado for garnish, with tortilla chips on the side. Serves 6.

Something on the Side

 *Jalapeño pepper*

Here are some recipes for side dishes to go with your chili or to accompany other meals.

Baked Papaya and Bananas

This dish can be served as a vegetable like candied yams or as a dessert topped with whipped cream or ice cream.

1 medium papaya, firm,
  slightly unripe
3 large bananas, firm, green tipped
3/4 cup brown sugar

1/4 teaspoon nutmeg
1/2 teaspoon cinnamon
1/4 cup butter, melted

Halve and peel papaya, removing seeds. Slice into sections. Peel bananas and cut into lengthwise strips. Place papaya sections and banana slices in greased baking dish. Mix brown sugar with nutmeg and cinnamon and sprinkle over papaya and bananas. Pour melted butter over brown sugar mixture. Bake in a 350-degree oven for 25 to 30 minutes. Makes 4 to 6 servings.

Charro Beans (Spanish Cowboy Beans)

This bean recipe is a classic and comes from the ranching areas of northern Mexico.

1 pound dried pinto beans
2 large onions, chopped
6 cloves garlic, minced
4 or 5 fresh jalapeños, seeded and diced
4 to 5 slices bacon, chopped

4 ripe tomatoes, chopped
1 chicken bouillon cube
1/2 cup cilantro leaves, minced
Salt to taste

Rinse beans under hot water for 3 or 4 minutes. Place in large sauce pan along with the onions, garlic, jalapeños, bacon, and chopped tomatoes. Cover with hot water and bring to boil. Lower heat. Simmer for 2 to 2-1/2 hours or until beans are tender. Add the chicken bouillon cube and chopped cilantro. Add salt to taste. Cook for 30 minutes more or until beans are done. Serve in a bowl with the broth or as a side for chili. Makes 6 to 8 servings.

Fried Green Tomatoes with Molasses Dressing

Fried green tomatoes are an old southern dish, a way to use up excess tomatoes from the garden. Try this recipe with excess garden tomatoes.

4 large green baseball-sized tomatoes
1 cup cornmeal
1 tablespoon ground cumin
Salt and pepper to taste
1 cup oil for frying

Dressing:
2/3 cup oil
Juice of 2 limes
2 tablespoons molasses
2 tablespoons cider vinegar
3 tablespoons chopped cilantro
1 teaspoon garlic powder
1 fresh jalapeño, seeded and minced
Salt and pepper to taste

Core tomatoes and cut each into 5 slices, about 1/2-inch thick. Mix cornmeal, cumin, salt and pepper. Dredge the tomato slices in the cornmeal mixture, shaking to remove excess.

Use large skillet and heat oil to hot, but not smoking. Working in batches, add half the tomato slices and fry until golden; about 2 minutes on each side. Drain on paper towels. Cook the remaining tomato slices. Combine dressing ingredients, mixing well. Place tomatoes on platter and pour dressing over the slices and serve. Makes 6 servings.

Frijoles

This is a basic recipe for cooking pinto beans.

3 cups pinto beans
1 clove garlic, minced
3 slices bacon, diced

4 quarts water
Salt

Rinse beans and soak overnight. Drain beans and place in large pot. Add garlic and diced bacon and cover with water. Bring to a boil and cover and simmer 1-1/2 to 2 hours or until beans are tender, adding more water as needed. When beans are soft, add salt to taste and cook 10 minutes more. The beans can also be cooked in a slow cooker following the cooker's instructions. Makes 6 to 8 servings. Reserve pinto bean liquid if you are making *Frijoles Refritos* on p. 121.

Frijoles Refritos

This recipe tastes best if using beans cooked a day or two earlier. This is the classic Mexican-style bean paste, so easy to make and so tasty.

2 tablespoons oil or bacon drippings
2 cups day old cooked pinto beans

Pinto bean liquid as needed
3/4 cup grated Cheddar cheese

Heat 2 tablespoons oil or bacon drippings in a heavy skillet. Add 2 cups day old cooked pinto beans. Use a potato masher and mash the beans as they cook; add some of the bean liquid to thin down as needed. When beans are mashed and heated through, place in ovenproof dish and sprinkle 3/4 cup grated cheese on top. Place in hot 400-degree oven until cheese melts, about 5 minutes. Serves 4.

Homemade Picante Sauce

This easy recipe is handy for a bumper crop of tomatoes and jalapeños in the garden.

2 quarts ripe tomatoes	3 tablespoons canning salt
2 cups whole jalapeños, caps removed	1 tablespoon ground cumin
2 cups chopped onions	1/2 cup sugar
1 tablespoon garlic powder	2 cups red wine vinegar

Plunge tomatoes into boiling water to loosen skins. Drop into cool water. When cool, remove skins, cut out stem and quarter tomatoes. Place first four ingredients in food processor and chop; do not over process. You may have to work in two batches. Combine all ingredients in large heavy saucepan. Boil, stirring frequently and skim off foam. Reduce heat and simmer for 1 hour, stirring frequently. Remove from heat, cool. Pour into hot sterilized canning jars and seal. Place jars in hot water bath and process for 35 to 40 minutes. Makes 4 pints.

Macaroni and Cheese Mexicana

2 cups medium elbow macaroni
1 teaspoon salt
1/2 cup butter
3 tablespoons flour
1/2 onion, finely minced
1 clove garlic, finely minced
1/2 teaspoon pepper

1 (4-ounce) can diced green chiles
1 tablespoon chopped pickled jalapeño
3 cups milk
1-1/2 cups grated sharp Cheddar cheese
1-1/2 cups grated Monterey Jack cheese
1 cup crushed tortilla chips
Paprika

Cook macaroni in boiling, salted water until tender but firm. Drain. In medium saucepan, melt butter and add flour, cooking until smooth. Stir to prevent burning. Add the next 5 ingredients. Cook on low, stirring constantly for about two
(continued)

Macaroni and Cheese Mexicana *(continued)*

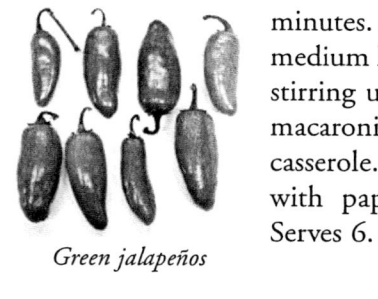

Green jalapeños

minutes. Add milk slowly, stirring until smooth. Cook on medium heat until thick. Remove and add grated cheeses, stirring until melted. Salt and pepper to taste. Combine macaroni and cheese sauce. Pour into a 2-1/2 quart casserole. Top with crushed tortilla chips and sprinkle with paprika. Bake at 350 degrees for 25 minutes. Serves 6.

Monterey and Green Chile Rice

1 cup rice, uncooked
2 cups sour cream

1 (4-ounce) can chopped green chiles
8 ounces Monterey Jack cheese, grated

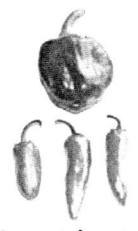

Cook rice according to package directions. Mix the cooked rice, sour cream and green chiles. Place in buttered baking dish and top with the grated cheese. Bake in a 350-degree oven for 30 minutes. Serves 4 to 6.

*Green jalapeños and
a habañero pepper*

Pan-fried Corn and Peppers

This recipe is so easy and it tastes so good. I started pan frying fresh corn when my kids were in braces and could not eat corn on the cob. Pan frying keeps that fresh corn taste.

2 tablespoons olive oil
Corn cut from 3 ears of fresh corn
  (about 2 cups)
1/2 cup finely chopped red bell pepper

1 jalapeño pepper, stemmed and
  seeded, minced fine
1/4 cup water
Salt and pepper to taste

Heat oil in heavy skillet; add corn, bell pepper and jalapeño pepper. Cook and stir. When heated through, add the water. Simmer until water cooks away and corn starts to brown. Season with salt and pepper. Makes 4 to 6 servings.

Sazón® Rice

This recipe makes beautiful orange rice and smells so good when cooking.

1-1/2 cups long grain rice
2 tablespoons oil
1/2 onion, chopped
3 cloves garlic, minced

3 cups chicken stock
2 packets Goya Sazón® Seasoning
1/2 cup frozen English peas
1 lime, sliced in half

Soak rice in bowl of hot water for 15 minutes. Drain rice in large strainer and rinse in cold water until water runs clear. Allow rice to drain for 10 minutes. Shake strainer to remove excess water. Heat oil in heavy skillet. Add the rice and stir and cook until rice begins to take on a golden color. Add the chopped onions

(continued)

Sazón® Rice   *(continued)*

and continue stirring and cooking until rice is golden brown. Add the garlic and cook a minute more or until the garlic releases its aroma. Stir in the chicken stock, one of Sazón® packets and the peas. Lower heat, and let simmer until rice is cooked and liquid almost absorbed. Only stir a little; add a little liquid if needed. When rice is cooked, add last packet of Sazón®, stir lightly so some of the orange color will be uneven. Squeeze the lime over the rice and let stand 5 minutes before serving. Makes 6 to 8 servings.

Peas

Texas-style Squash and Corn

This is a favorite Texas vegetable dish usually made with the Mexican squash called *calabacitas* which is closely related to zucchini.

2 tablespoons oil
1 small onion, chopped
1 clove garlic
4 small *calabacitas* or zucchini, sliced

1 (4-ounce) can chopped green chiles
2 cups fresh or frozen corn
Salt and pepper to taste
1/2 cup grated Cheddar cheese

Heat oil and brown onion, garlic and *calabacitas*. Discard garlic clove. Add green chiles and corn. Season with salt and pepper. Cook a few minutes. Add cheese, mixing well. Serves 4.

Take a Can of Chili

Chili was first canned in the 1880s in San Antonio as food for the U. S. Army. One of the most successful canned chili operations started in the back of a meat market in Corsicana, Texas, in the 1920s when Lyman Davis first made his Wolf® brand chili, named for his pet wolf, Kaiser Bill. You would think Texans would eat the most canned chili. According to food writer and chili expert, W. C. Jameson, more canned chili is sold in New York City than in the entire state of Texas.

Once chili in a can became a common grocery store staple, it didn't take long for Texas cooks to come up with new ways to use this handy food. This section is devoted to canned chili recipes.

Chili Cheese Dip

2 (8-ounce) packages cream
cheese
1 (16-ounce) can chili (no beans)
1 cup grated Cheddar cheese

1 bunch green onions, chopped
1 (4-ounce) can sliced black olives,
drained
Sliced pickled jalapeños to taste

Spread cream cheese on bottom of large platter. Heat chili and pour over cream
cheese. Sprinkle on Cheddar cheese, then the green onions and black olive slices.
Garnish with jalapeño slices. Serve immediately with tortilla chips. Makes 10 to
12 servings.

Chili Joes

Here's an easy Tex-Mex version of the popular Sloppy Joe sandwich.

1 pound lean ground beef
1 small onion, chopped
1 (16-ounce) can chili

1 pickled jalapeño, chopped
6 hamburger buns, toasted
Corn tortilla chips

Brown the beef and onion in a heavy skillet. Add the chili and cook until hot. Stir in the chopped jalapeños. Serve on toasted buns with tortilla chips on the side. Makes 4 to 6 servings.

Green jalapeño

Chili Mac

This budget-wise recipe is an old family favorite, easy to make and a kid pleaser.

1 package elbow macaroni
2 (16-ounce) cans chili

1 large onion, chopped
2 cups grated Cheddar cheese

Cook macaroni according to package instructions. Drain and place in greased casserole dish. Pour chili and chopped onions over macaroni, stirring to mix. Sprinkle cheese on top and bake in a 375-degree oven for 15 to 20 minutes or until cheese is melted and chili is heated through. Makes 8 servings.

Chili Vegetable Soup

1 medium-sized box or bag
   frozen vegetables
1 medium onion, diced
2 stalks celery, chopped
2 potatoes, peeled and diced

1 (15-ounce) can chili
4 cups water or stock
1 (15-ounce) can tomatoes
Salt and pepper to taste

Using large pot, barely cover potatoes, onions and celery with water and bring to boil; cook until almost tender, about ten minutes. Add frozen vegetables and cook 5 minutes more. Add chili, water or stock and canned tomatoes. Simmer for 25 to 30 minutes. Season with salt and pepper. Serves 4 to 6.

Classic Frito Pie

2-1/2 cups Fritos® Original Corn
   Chips, divided
1 small onion, chopped

1-1/2 cups grated Cheddar cheese
1 (16-ounce) can chili

Heat chili in saucepan. Spread 1-1/2 cups of the Fritos® in the bottom of a shallow baking dish, sprinkle with the chopped onion and half the Cheddar cheese. Pour heated chili over the mixture. Sprinkle the remaining Fritos® over the chili and top with the remaining cheese. Bake in a 350-degree oven for 10 to 15 minutes. Makes 4 to 6 servings.

Mexican Hominy

1 (15-ounce) can yellow hominy, drained
1 (15-ounce) can white hominy, drained
1 medium onion, chopped
1 (15-ounce) can chili (no beans)
1 cup grated Cheddar cheese

Place drained hominy in greased casserole dish. Pour chili over the hominy and top with the grated cheese. Bake in a 375-degree oven until cheese is melted, about 15 minutes. Serves 6 to 8.

Rancho Eggs

1 (15-ounce) can chili (no beans)
1/2 onion, chopped
4 eggs

1 cup grated Longhorn Cheddar
cheese

Heat chili in saucepan, add chopped onions and cook a few minutes. Pour chili mixture into shallow baking dish. Make 4 holes in the chili mixture and crack eggs and drop them into the holes. Sprinkle cheese over the top of the casserole. Bake in a 325-degree oven for 15 to 20 minutes or until eggs are set. Serve with avocado slices and warm flour tortillas. Makes 2 to 4 servings.

Texas Hash

2 tablespoons oil
1 onion, chopped
1 green bell pepper, seeded and
   chopped
1 (15-ounce) can diced tomatoes

4 cups cooked rice
1 (15-ounce) can chili (no beans)
1 cup grated Cheddar cheese
Salt and pepper to taste

Heat oil in skillet, add onions and bell pepper and cook until onions are limp. Add tomatoes, rice, and chili, mixing well. Pour mixture into greased baking dish and top with grated cheese. Bake in a 375-degree oven for 15 to 20 minutes. Makes 6 servings.

Tex-Mex Cabbage Rolls

1 (15-ounce) can chili
2 cups cooked rice
1 small onion, diced
1 tablespoon salt in large pot of water
1 small head cabbage

1 (15-ounce) can diced tomatoes
1/2 cup water
2 tablespoons vinegar
1/4 cup brown sugar
1 teaspoon salt

Mix chili, rice, and onion in bowl and set aside. Bring large pot of water and salt to a boil. Peel off outer leaves of the cabbage and drop into boiling water, cooking until wilted, about 5 minutes. Drain leaves and allow to cool. Place 2 tablespoons of the chili/rice mixture on each cabbage leaf, fold over edges and roll up tightly. Place cabbage rolls seam side down in buttered baking dish. Mix tomatoes, water, vinegar, brown sugar, and salt and pour over the cabbage rolls. Bake in a 325-degree oven 35 to 40 minutes. Makes 6 to 8 servings.

Tex-Mex Twice Baked Potatoes

6 large baked potatoes, pulp removed
   and mashed
1 (4-ounce) can chopped green chiles
1/4 cup finely chopped onion
1/2 cup butter, melted

1 cup sour cream
4 ounces Longhorn Cheddar cheese,
   grated
1 (16-ounce) can chili, no beans

Mix mashed potatoes, green chiles, onion, butter and sour cream. Fill potato shells with this mixture, pressing down to make room at top. Spoon on some chili and top with grated cheese. Bake in a 400-degree oven for 15 minutes. Serves 6.

Breads, Rolls, and Biscuits

Nothing goes better with chili than some hot cornbread or fry bread. Here are some simple recipes to try. The chili biscuit recipe is an old North Texas favorite, great to serve at cookouts.

Cheesy Beer Biscuits

A different beer biscuit and so easy to make.

4 cups Bisquick® or other biscuit mix
4 ounces sharp Cheddar cheese, grated

1 can beer, room temperature
1/4 cup sugar

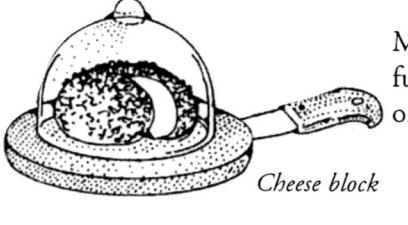

Cheese block

Mix all ingredients. Fill greased muffin tin 1/2 full. Bake in a 400-degree oven for 15 minutes or until well browned. Makes 24 biscuits.

Lucille's Famous Chili Biscuits

This recipe is an adaptation from a recipe from Lucille Bishop Smith, a legendary caterer and food educator from Fort Worth, Texas. The chili biscuits were her most famous food product and were sold frozen in North Texas grocery stores in the 1960s and 1970s. Smith also developed the first commercial hot roll mix sold in grocery stores so, as a tribute to her, I am using a hot roll mix for this recipe.

Make the Chili for Chili Biscuits on p. 145 in advance. Use this chili recipe for making the chili biscuits; do not try to substitute canned chili or another chili recipe.

Chili Biscuits

1 box of hot roll mix
8 ounces grated American cheese

One batch of
    Chili for Chili Biscuits p. 145

Make roll dough according to package instructions and let rise for first time until double in bulk. Punch down and place on floured board and knead for a few minutes. Then roll dough to 1/2" thickness and cut biscuits with 1-1/2" cutter. Place on oiled cookie sheet, brush with melted butter. Cover and let rise for 20 to 30 minutes or until double. Bake 15 to 20 minutes in 450-degree oven. Remove from oven, brush with melted butter and allow to cool. When cool, cut a marble size ball from top of each biscuit using a melon ball cutter. Fill with chili made for "Chili Biscuits." Top with a tablespoon of grated American cheese. Heat at 350 degrees for 5 minutes. Serve hot. Makes 2-1/2 to 3 dozen biscuits.

Chili for Chili Biscuits

2-1/2 pounds lean ground beef
1 large onion, finely chopped
1/4 cup vegetable shortening
1/4 cup chili powder
2 tablespoons ground cumin
2 teaspoons salt

2 teaspoons pepper
1 tablespoon garlic powder
1 tablespoon paprika
1 tablespoon Accent®
3 cups boiling water

Put the ground beef into heavy saucepan with tight fitting lid. Cover and cook on low, in its own juices, stirring often until tender (about 40 minutes). In separate pan sauté the onions in the shortening. Add sautéed onions to the meat. Add the remaining seasonings, mixing well. Pour in the water and stir to mix. Cover and simmer for 20 minutes. Cool and refrigerate for future use.

Cornmeal Biscuits

1-3/4 cups all purpose flour
3/4 cup yellow cornmeal
3 teaspoons baking powder
2 tablespoons sugar

1/2 teaspoon salt
1/2 cup (1 stick) unsalted butter, cut
  into small pieces
2/3 cup milk

Sift flour, cornmeal, baking powder, sugar and salt into large bowl. Work the butter into the flour mixture until it is mealy. Stir in the milk to make a sticky dough. Place dough on floured board and knead for 1 minute. Pat or roll out dough to a thickness of 1/2-inch, adding flour as needed to prevent sticking. Cut with a 2-1/2-inch round biscuit cutter. Arrange biscuits one inch apart on lightly buttered baking sheet. Bake at 450 degrees for 10 to 12 minutes. Serve hot. Makes 12 to 15 biscuits.

Easy Jalapeño Cheese Bread

1 box hot roll mix

2 cups sharp Cheddar cheese, grated

1/4 cup finely diced pickled jalapeños

Prepare roll mix according to package directions. Knead dough until smooth (4 to 5 minutes). Place in greased bowl and cover with tea towel. Let rise in warm place until doubled in bulk (30 to 45 minutes). Punch down dough and knead for two minutes. Pat or roll out dough into a rectangle, about 9 x 15 inches. Sprinkle the cheese and the jalapeños over the dough. Fold dough over and knead. Repeat this several times. The cheese will not fully incorporate into the dough. Roll dough up tightly and pinch the ends of the dough to seal. Place open edge down on greased baking sheet and cover with tea towel. Let rise in warm place until doubled (about 20 to 25 minutes). Bake in a 375-degree oven until browned (about 25 to 30 minutes). Test by thumping bottom, it should have a hollow sound when done. Cool on wire baking rack.

Homemade Crackers

4 cups flour, sifted
1 tablespoon salt
1 tablespoon sugar

1/4 cup butter
1 cup milk

Sift dry ingredients together. Cut in butter until mixture feels mealy. Stir in milk and mix to make a stiff dough. Let rest in refrigerator for 20 minutes. Roll out to 1/4" thick on floured board and cut into 2-inch squares or other shapes. Place on greased cookie sheet and pierce each piece several times with a fork. Bake in a 400-degree oven until golden brown, about 15 minutes. Makes 4 to 5 dozen crackers. Store in tightly closed container.

Jalapeño Cornbread

1 cup yellow cornmeal
1 cup flour
1 tablespoon baking powder
1/2 teaspoon salt
1 tablespoon sugar
1 small (8-1/2-ounce) can cream-style corn

1 cup milk
1/4 cup vegetable oil
2 eggs, beaten
1 cup grated sharp Cheddar cheese
1/4 cup minced pickled or fresh jalapeño

Heat heavy iron skillet or muffin pans in 375-degree oven. In large bowl, combine first 5 ingredients. Make a hole in the center of the cornmeal mixture and pour in the cream corn, milk, oil and eggs. Stir to barely mix. Add grated cheese

(continued)

Jalapeño Cornbread *(continued)*

and jalapeños, stirring to mix; do not overbeat. Remove hot skillet or muffin pans from oven and spray with non-stick baking spray. Pour in batter and place in oven, baking until top is brown (15 to 20 minutes). Heating the baking pan in advance will make the cornbread bake faster and put a crisp golden crust on the bottom of the bread.

Jalapeño peppers

Navajo Fry Bread

For a true Southwestern meal, make a batch of *chili verde* and serve with fry bread.

3 cups flour
1 teaspoon salt
1 tablespoon baking powder

1 cup warm water (approximately)
Oil for frying

In large bowl, mix the flour, salt, and baking powder. Make a hole in the center and pour in the water. Start stirring and work the flour into the liquid. Keep stirring until all the flour is incorporated. You should have soft, sticky dough. Turn out on floured board and knead for about 5 minutes. Cover and let dough rest for about 20 minutes. Divide the dough into 8 balls. Roll each ball out into a disk about 1/4-inch thick. Fry in hot oil and drain on paper towels. Serves 8.

New Mexico Blue Corn Muffins

1 egg, beaten
1 cup milk
2 tablespoons melted butter
1/2 cup blue cornmeal

3/4 cup flour
2 tablespoons sugar
1-1/2 teaspoons baking powder
1/2 teaspoon salt

In large mixing bowl, combine the egg, milk, melted butter and blue cornmeal. Let stand for 10 minutes to soften the cornmeal. Sift flour, sugar, baking powder, and salt together in another bowl. Give the blue cornmeal mixture a stir and add the flour mixture, stirring gently to combine. Place batter in greased 12-cup muffin pan, filling each cup half full. Bake in a preheated 400-degree oven for 12 to 15 minutes or until muffins are browned on top. Remove from oven and allow to cool in muffin pan for 5 minutes before removing. Makes 12 muffins.

Onion Batter Bread

3-1/4 cups all purpose flour
2 packages dry yeast
2 tablespoons sugar
1 teaspoon salt

1/4 cup butter, melted
1 cup chopped onion
1-1/4 cups warm water
1 egg

In large mixing bowl, combine half the flour, all the yeast, sugar and salt. Mix well. Sauté onion in butter until limp and clear, add to flour mixture. Add water and egg. Stir and mix well, beat for about 3 minutes. Gradually add in the remaining flour until you have a stiff batter. Pour into a greased 2-quart casserole dish. Cover and let rise in a warm place until doubled in bulk (about 1 hour). Heat oven to 375 degrees. Bake the bread for 35 to 40 minutes until well browned. Remove from oven and brush top with melted butter. Remove from pan and serve warm or cold.

Quick Herbed Biscuits

1/4 cup butter, melted
1-1/2 teaspoons parsley flakes
1 teaspoon dill seed

1/2 teaspoon garlic powder
1/2 cup fresh grated Parmesan cheese
1 can refrigerated biscuits

Pour melted butter into 9" pie dish. Add parsley, dill seed, garlic powder and Parmesan cheese, mixing well. Cut each refrigerator biscuit into quarters and turn each piece over in the melted butter mixture to coat, arranging the pieces on pie plate so they will touch. Bake in a 425-degree oven for 12 to 15 minutes.

Something Sweet

Peach

After eating your fill of chili, it's time to have dessert. In keeping with the simple nature of chili, these dessert recipes are easy to make, but taste so good.

Banana Fritters

1-1/2 cups flour
2 teaspoons baking powder
2 tablespoons powdered sugar
1/4 teaspoon salt
1 egg, beaten

2/3 cup milk
Oil for frying
3 bananas, mashed
Powdered sugar

Sift flour, baking powder, powdered sugar, and salt together in large bowl. Add egg and milk together, then add to flour mixture. Fold in bananas. If mixture is too thin, add more flour, if mixture is too thick, add more milk. Pour oil to a depth of 1-inch in heavy skillet and heat until hot. Drop batter by teaspoonfuls into hot oil. Brown on one side, then turn to brown other side. Drain on paper towels. Dust with powdered sugar. Serves 4 to 6.

Cajun Chess Pie

1/4 cup cocoa
1-1/2 cups sugar
2 eggs
1/2 cup chopped pecans
1/4 cup melted butter

1/2 cup evaporated milk
1/2 cup shredded coconut
1 teaspoon vanilla
1 (9-inch) pie shell, unbaked

Preheat oven to 400 degrees. Mix cocoa and sugar in bowl until no lumps remain. Add other ingredients. Pour into the unbaked pie shell and bake for 30 minutes. Serve with whipped cream or vanilla ice cream.

Carrot Pineapple Sheet Cake

2 cups plain flour
2 cups sugar
2 teaspoons baking soda
1 teaspoon salt
2 teaspoons cinnamon
1-1/2 cups oil

4 eggs
2-1/2 cups grated carrots
1 (8-1/2-ounce) can crushed
 pineapple, undrained
3/4 cup chopped pecans

Stir and mix dry ingredients. Add oil and blend well. Add eggs, one at a time, stirring after each addition. Add carrots, pineapple and nuts, mixing well. Pour in a 10" x 14" x 2" pan that has been buttered and lightly floured. Bake in a 325-degree oven for 40 to 45 minutes until top springs back when touched. When cool, frost with Gooey Frosting on p. 164.

Chewy Oatmeal Chocolate Chip Cookies

1 cup butter
1 cup white sugar
1 cup brown sugar
2 eggs
1 teaspoon vanilla
1-1/2 cups flour

1 teaspoon salt
1 teaspoon soda
3 cups oatmeal
1 cup shredded coconut
1 (6-ounce) package
   semi-sweet chocolate chips

Cream butter and sugars together, add eggs and vanilla, mixing well. Sift flour, salt, and soda together and add to creamed mixture. Add oatmeal and coconut and mix well, then stir in the chocolate chips. Drop by teaspoonfuls on cookie sheet which is lined with parchment paper or well greased. Bake in a 400-degree oven for 8 to 10 minutes. Watch because these cookies brown very fast. Let stand about 5 minutes before removing from cookie sheet. Makes about 7 dozen.

Chocolate Butter Cream Icing

1/3 cup butter
3 cups powdered sugar
1/3 cup cocoa
Pinch of salt

1 teaspoon vanilla
3 tablespoons milk or black coffee
1/2 cup walnuts

Mix all ingredients except walnuts until smooth. Frost cake p. 161 with icing and top with toasted walnuts.

Toasted Walnuts: Place 1/2 cup broken walnut meats in ungreased pan. Bake in oven at 325 degrees for 12 to 15 minutes, stirring 2 or 3 times while baking to prevent burning. Make enough to have a 1/2 cup of shelled walnuts.

Cocoa Sheet Cake with Toasted Walnuts

3/4 cup butter
1-3/4 cups sugar
2 eggs
1 teaspoon vanilla
3/4 cup unsweetened cocoa

2 cups flour
1-1/4 teaspoons baking soda
1/2 teaspoon salt
1-1/3 cups water

Cream butter and sugar until light and fluffy. Add eggs and vanilla, beat one minute at medium speed. Combine flour, cocoa, baking soda, and salt and sift together. Add alternately with water to the creamed mixture. Pour batter into 9 x 13-inch greased and floured sheet cake pan. Bake at 350 degrees for 20 to 25 minutes or until top springs back when touched. Frost with icing on p. 160.

Devil's Cobbler and Sauce

Here's an old favorite that is easy to make. Part cake, part sauce, with a rich chocolate taste. Serve warm from the oven, topped with a dollop of whipped cream — yum, yum!

1 cup flour
1/2 teaspoon salt
3/4 cup sugar
2 teaspoons baking powder
3 tablespoons cocoa
1/2 cup milk
2 tablespoons melted butter
1 teaspoon vanilla

1/2 cup nuts (optional)
Whipped cream or ice cream

Devil's Cobbler Sauce:
1/2 cup sugar
1/2 cup brown sugar
5 tablespoons cocoa
1 cup hot water

Combine dry ingredients. Add milk, butter, vanilla and nuts (optional). Pour into greased 8" square pan. Add Devil's Cobbler Sauce before baking.

Devil's Cobbler Sauce: Combine sugars and cocoa, mixing well. Add hot water and stir until blended. Pour over Devil's Cobbler ingredients already in pan.

Bake in a 350-degree oven for 40 minutes. Serve warm, topped with whipped cream or ice cream. Serves 6 to 8.

Gooey Frosting

1/2 stick butter
1 (3-ounce) package cream cheese
3 cups powdered sugar

Fresh orange sections, chopped
Juice from 1 lemon

Cream butter and cream cheese. Add powdered sugar, orange sections, and lemon juice. Mix well, trying to keep from squeezing the juice from the orange sections. Frosting will be runny and gooey. Spread on cooled cake.

Lemon Cake Pie

1-1/2 cups sugar
1/2 cup flour
1/2 cup butter, melted
1/4 teaspoon salt

3 eggs, separated
Juice and grated peel from 3 lemons
1-1/2 cups milk
1 (9-inch) unbaked pie shell

Combine the sugar, flour, butter, salt, and egg yolks. Beat until smooth and creamy. Add lemon juice and peel and mix well. Add milk, mixing slowly. Beat egg whites until stiff but not dry and fold into lemon mixture. Bake empty pie shell in 350-degree oven for 5 minutes. Pour in filling and bake for 40 minutes or until filling is firm. When pie is cut there will be a cake layer on top of the pie filling. Garnish with whipped cream and sliced strawberries.

Moist Pineapple-Coconut Sheet Cake

1 box yellow cake mix
4 eggs
3/4 cup oil
1/2 (20-ounce) can crushed pineapple
   with juice, divided
1 teaspoon almond extract

Icing:
1-3/4 cups powdered sugar
1/4 cup (1/2 stick) butter
Remainder of pineapple
1-1/2 cups coconut

Preheat oven to 325 degrees. Butter and flour a 9 x 13-inch baking pan. Mix first 5 ingredients together. Beat for 3 minutes at medium speed. Bake for 35 minutes or until done. As soon as the cake is removed from the oven, prick all over with a fork. Mix icing ingredients together and spread on the cake while the cake is still warm. Allow to cool for 30 to 45 minutes. Sprinkle entire cake with coconut, gently pressing the coconut into the icing. Keep cake covered to stay nice and moist. Serves 12.

Orange Chocolate Chippers

My mother took this from the Recipe of the Month section of a women's magazine back in the 1950s. It has been a family favorite ever since. I'd double or triple the recipe because these cookies won't last long.

1 cup shortening (do not substitute butter or margarine)
1 cup sugar
1 (3-ounce) package cream cheese
2 eggs
2 teaspoons vanilla extract

2 tablespoons finely chopped and grated orange peel
2 cups sifted flour
1 teaspoon salt
1 (6-ounce) package semi-sweet chocolate chips

(continued)

Orange Chocolate Chippers *(continued)*

Cream shortening, sugar, and cream cheese together. Stir in eggs, one at a time. Add vanilla and orange peel. Mix well. Sift flour and salt together. Add to creamed mixture. Add the chocolate chips and mix well. Drop by teaspoonfuls, 2-inches apart on well-greased cookie sheets. Bake at 350 degrees for 12 minutes or until edge of cookies just start to brown. Place on cake rack to cool. Makes about 3 dozen.

Watch closely as these cookies burn easily. Also, shiny cookie sheets work best, as they do not brown as quickly. If you have dark cookie sheets, line them with aluminum foil or parchment paper when baking these cookies.

Peach Custard Cake

1-1/2 cups flour
1/2 teaspoon salt
1/2 cup butter or margarine
1 large can sliced peaches, drained
    and reserve 1/2 cup of syrup

1/2 cup sugar mixed with
    1/2 teaspoon cinnamon
1 egg
1 cup evaporated milk

Preheat oven to 350 degrees. Mix flour, salt, and margarine with a pastry blender or fingers. Press mixture firmly on bottom and half way up sides of 8-inch square baking dish, which has been buttered. Arrange well-drained peaches on crust in pan. Sprinkle cinnamon-sugar mixture over peaches. Bake 20 minutes. Mix the reserved peach syrup, the egg and evaporated milk. Pour over peaches and bake 30 minutes more or until custard is firm except in center. Center becomes firm upon standing. Serve warm or cold.

Peanut Butter Brownies

1 cup flour
1 teaspoon baking powder
1/2 teaspoon salt
1/2 cup sugar
1/2 cup firm packed brown sugar
1/2 cup (1 stick) melted butter

2 eggs
1 teaspoon vanilla
2/3 cup crunchy peanut butter
1/3 cup finely chopped cocktail peanuts
1/2 package (11 ounces)
  butterscotch chips

Preheat oven to 350 degrees. Butter a 9 x 13-inch baking pan. Sift flour, baking powder, and salt together, set aside. In a large mixing bowl, place sugars and melted butter; mix well. Stir in 2 eggs and vanilla, then blend in the peanut butter. Add flour mixture, stirring well. Add chopped peanuts and butterscotch chips, stir. Spread mixture in pan. Bake for 20 to 22 minutes until edges are lightly browned. Do not overcook. Allow to cool 3 hours, then cut into bars. Makes 30 bars.

Beverages

Here's a few recipes both with and without alcohol. All are easy to make and so sure to please.

Border Buttermilk

1 (6-ounce) can frozen lemonade   1 (6-ounce) juice can tequila
1 (6-ounce) juice can pineapple juice   2 cups crushed ice

Place in blender and blend until ice is crushed and drink is slushy. Makes 6 drinks.

Sparkling Limeade

5 or 6 large limes   1/3 to 1/2 cup sugar
1 quart club soda

Squeeze juice from all limes except one. Pour juice into a glass pitcher. Cut remaining lime into very thin slices and add to pitcher. Add club soda and sweeten with sugar to taste. Serve in tall glasses over ice cubes. Makes 4 servings.

Chocolate Shakes

1 cup nonfat dry milk
1/4 cup water

1/3 cup chocolate syrup
2 cups ice cubes

Place ingredients in blender and blend until ice is crushed. Makes 2 shakes.

Strawberry Yogurt Shakes

2 cups fresh or frozen strawberries
1/2 cup nonfat dry milk
1/2 cup plain yogurt

1/4 cup honey
1/2 teaspoon vanilla
3/4 cup ice cubes

Place ingredients in blender and blend until ice is crushed. Makes 2 shakes.

Frozen Peach Daiquiris

1 large ripe peach or 3 tablespoons
    frozen peaches
3 tablespoons frozen limeade
    concentrate

2/3 cup light rum
6 ice cubes or more

Peach

Place all ingredients in a blender and blend until ice is crushed. Serve immediately.
Makes 4 small drinks.

Old-fashioned Sherbet Punch

3 quarts chilled ginger ale   1 gallon orange or lime sherbet

Chill punch bowl in advance. Place sherbet in punch bowl and add ginger ale. Mix and serve immediately. You can add a cup or two of vodka if you want a more spirited punch. Serves 15 to 20.

Spiced Tea Mix

2 cups orange Tang® Drink Mix   1 teaspoon cinnamon
1/2 cup instant tea with lemon   1/2 teaspoon cloves
  and sweetener

Mix all ingredients and store in jar with tight lid. To make a cup of spiced tea, mix two teaspoons of the mix with 1 cup of boiling water.

Sangria

1 bottle dry red wine
1/2 cup brandy
3 tablespoons frozen lemonade
    concentrate
1/2 cup orange juice

1 orange, sliced
1 lemon, sliced
1 lime, sliced
1 cup club soda

In large glass pitcher, mix wine, brandy, lemonade concentrate, and orange juice. Add the fruit slices. Cover and refrigerate until ready to serve. Just before serving add the club soda. Pour into glasses over ice cubes, garnishing each glass with some of the fruit slices. Serves 6 to 8.

BOOKS BY MAIL Stocking Stuffers Postpaid You may mix titles. One book for $13.95; two for $23.00; three for $33.00; four for $40.00; six for $57.50; ten for $95.00. Prices subject to change.

Æbleskiver and More (Danish)
American Gothic Cookbook
Amish Mennonite Recipes
Buffets and Potlucks
Cherished Czech Recipes
Czech & Slovak Kolaches
Dandy Dutch Recipes
Dear Danish Recipes
Dutch Style Recipes
Fine Finnish Foods
Fire in the Bowl: Favorite Chili Recipes
French Recipes
German Style Recipes
Great German Recipes
Healthy Recipes

Hungarian Recipes
Microwave Recipes
Norwegian Centennial Recipes
Norwegian Recipes
Pleasing Polish Recipes
Quality Czech Mushroom Recipes
Quality Dumpling Recipes
Recipes from Ireland
Recipes from Old Mexico
Savory Scottish Recipes
Scandinavian Holiday Recipes
Scandinavian Smorgasbord Recipes
Scandinavian Style Fish and Seafood
Scandinavian Sweet Treats
Slavic Specialties

Slovak Recipes
Splendid Swedish Recipes
Tales from Texas Tables
Texas Cookoff
Time-Honored Norwegian Recipes
Ukrainian Recipes
Waffles, Flapjacks, Pancakes, from Scandinavia and Around the World

License to Cook Series:
Alaska Style; Arizona Style; Colorado Style; Florida Style; Iowa Style; Italian Style; Minnesota Style; Missouri Style; New Mexico Style; Oregon Style; Texas Style; and Wisconsin Style

Penfield Books, 215 Brown Street, Iowa City, IA 52245-5801 • 1-800-728-9998 • www.penfieldbooks.com

Chile *Ristra* over Organ Mountains

One ristra *(an arrangement of drying chile pepper pods) hangs under a portal with decorative* corbels. *Featured in the background are the rugged Organ Mountains of New Mexico. The tallest peak reaches 9,012 feet.*

Woodcut by ©Esther Feske 2010